THE
ART OF
WAR

THE
ART OF
WAR

WITH STUDY GUIDE
BY THERESA PUSKAR

SUN TZU

LIONEL GILES
TRANSLATION

MEDIA

MEDIA

Published 2018 by Gildan Media LLC
aka G&D Media
www.GandDmedia.com

FIRST EDITION 2018

Front Cover design by David Rheinhardt of Pyrographx

Interior design by Meghan Day Healey of Story Horse, LLC

Library of Congress Cataloging-in-Publication Data is available upon request

ISBN: 978-1-7225-0007-8

10   9   8   7   6   5   4   3   2   1

Contents

Contents

Foreword

The *Art of War* is a text that has withstood the test of time. It is the oldest military treatise in the world. Believed to have been written over 2,400 years ago by Sun Tzu during the 6th century B.C., it has been translated, referenced, studied, and practiced by everything from military leaders to present-day self-help experts the world-over. While war strategies have been practiced and recorded throughout time, this particular document is still being used in the 21st century. Why?

Sun Tzu's text of principles and practices carries with it wise truths that span the full spectrum of life disciplines. It has been referenced by scholars and experts alike, many who have spawned strategic and self-help books, using it as their core body of research. Texts have been written spanning a myriad of subjects—everything from warfare and business leadership, to courtship strategies and relationship-building. The fact that its contents are so broad in their potential application is a testament to this text. It indicates that it is rich with wisdom and that there is more to it than basic military maneuvering. In fact, some scholars claim that the staying power of this ancient text is largely due to the fact that its wisdom does not lie in sword fighting strategies and strategic maneuvering of armies, but in its mental power. Inherent within it is wisdom that far outreaches time and space.

I usually suggest that you read the book first, and then during your second read-thru, take the time to go through the Study Guide. In this case, however, I suggest that you work through the Study Guide in tandem with the treatise text. Without relating Sun Tzu's text to a particular area of your life in which you are struggling, it will be difficult for you to gain its full impact and benefits.

One of the stories I heard most when researching this book exemplifies just how committed to his word Sun Tzu was. At one point in his military career, he was challenged by Ho Lu, King of Wu to test his leadership skills, integrity and word. The king asked if he could submit his theory on managing soldiers to a slight test. He was asked if he could command anyone, including women. He asserted that he could. Thus, the king asked him to command many of his concubines. To start, Sun Tzu had difficulty guiding the women through the military drills. As he asserted his directives, they did not obey, and simply giggled. As any honorable general would, he blamed himself. Sun Tzu tried again, but again they did not follow his directions. In response to their disobedience, he ordered that the two leaders of the companies be beheaded. Once the king saw that his favorite concubines were about to be beheaded, he tried to put an end to the test, however Sun Tzu continued to follow through on his command. The two were beheaded. On seeing how committed he was, the women realized their lives were in danger, and proceeded to obey him. In the end, the concubines followed Sun Tzu's commands with precision and form. The king saw Sun Tzu's prowess and commitment to his word, and thereby made him general of his army.

I would encourage you dig deep into the inherent wisdom of this powerful text. As was modeled by Sun Tzu in this provocative story, it takes commitment, discipline and perseverance, but in the end, his strategies are solid and the insights are profound.

Winning the Internal Battle

While there have been many Study Guides that were seeded by the tenets of *The Art of War*, the battle that we will focus on in this manual is the war that begins and ends all wars—the conflict within you. Modern psychology and ancient wisdom both point to the truth that turmoil that manifests in the outer world is a mirror of the struggles that we each face from within. In other words, the unrest within each of us is a microcosm for the greater battle that ensues in the world around us. Great masters share the insight that the best thing you could do to cure the world of warfare, is to heal the battle that continuously mounts within your mind. Taking the time to reflect and find the warrior within you that wishes to heal your inner battles once and for all, will not only serve you in your life, but will serve the world as a whole. For, everything you say, feel, think and do, leaves energetic footprints in the world. As you heal yourself, you heal the earth and its inhabitants.

For the purpose of this manual, it is vital that you face the warring factions that rest within you. If you reflect on any and all inner turmoil, it will be revealed to you that there are two opposing sides: Your highest self and your ego self. Your ego wears many armored masks. Apathy, resentment, defensiveness, criticism, righteousness and shame are a few of the more potent expressions. If you look deep into your ego, you will discover that its soldiers are terrified and wear thick protective armor to avoid dealing with their fears. The apathetic soldier would rather pretend nothing is wrong, while the resentful soldier lashes out at others and blames the world for his ails. The defensive soldier is constantly ready for attack, unable to receive feedback from anyone, and the critic finds fault in everyone and everything. The righteous soldier fools herself into believing that she is better than others, and the shameful soldier is filled with self-contempt. Each of these soldiers is your ego's warrior. They wear their armor well, and do so to try and protect you from yourself.

Let's take a look at one of your ego's most powerful soldiers—your inner critic. If you look at the root of so many of your life challenges, most often you will find your inner critic in the driver's seat. It finds fault in both you and in others. When others trigger you to the point of annoyance, your inner critic is at the heart of the matter—judging, condemning and creating animosity. The lack of compassion and acceptance it has of others is directly related to its condemnation of you. In other words, its response to others is an outer reflection of its inner judgments of you. The good news is that once you are able to understand your inner critic, you are more accepting of yourself and others. Your relationships will improve and your life will become more harmonious. For this reason, it is important that you constantly keep your inner critic and it's fellow ego warriors in the forefront of your consciousness as you do the exercises in the pages that follow. A great deal of the strategizing we will do will focus on the various faces of your ego. Your job is to recognize and understand those faces, so that you can combat them and shift your relationship with them once and for all.

It is important to note that it is not helpful to judge either of the two positions (higher-self and ego), nor the soldiers that are on the frontlines of each army. Like two nations at war, from within the hearts and minds of the two opposing positions, their reasoning is righteous and worthy. Each has its task and legitimate point of view. So it is with your highest self and your ego self. While your first instinct is to judge your ego, a great deal of the distress you are in is due to that judgment. You need to make peace with all of yourself—the good, the bad and the ugly. Then and only then will you be able to forge ahead in your life with a greater sense of peaceful joy and ease.

In this manual, you will spend time getting to know your opponent, for knowledge is power. Exploring and understanding the various aspects of your ego's armored clan is the first step towards making peace. Once you get to know them, then you will have the basic knowledge to lay out and follow through on your strategic plan. Staying focused, honest with yourself and committed will ensure victory on this heroic and noble personal battle.

Theresa Puskar
Writer, Study Guide

Preparation

Before delving into the wisdom of Sun Tzu's tenets, it is important that you are familiar with each of the two positions and why they continue to fight their ceaseless battles. While you may want to side with your higher self, the ego seeks as well to be your ally, as its intention is to protect you. It is on guard at the root of your being, and has been there since the beginning of time. It protects and responds to your basic needs. Thus, whenever you feel threatened, emotionally or physically, it will rear itself to protect you. As you begin to understand it and start to feel safe in the world, it will let down its guard and the battles will occur less and less frequently.

1. To start, write a list of at least five situations from early childhood to the present time, in which you have felt threatened or unsafe. You may have felt physically or emotionally attracted. List whom or what threatened you, and what you did or felt in response:

Situation #1   Response

Situation #2   Response

Situation #3   Response

Situation #4   Response

Situation #5   Response

2. Now go through the list that you created in #1. Reflect on each situation, as see how each has contributed to the heavy and mighty emotional armor that your ego has created to try to prevent future such pain.

3. Write a note of gratitude to your ego, for its valiant efforts to protect you. Then take some time to really feel into gratitude for its determination and commitment.

    Gratitude Note #1

    Gratitude Note #2

    Gratitude Note #3

    Gratitude Note #4

    Gratitude Note #5

4. The exercises you did in numbers 1 to 3 should have provided you with a greater sense of gratitude. They have opened a window so that you see into your ego self with greater clarity. You should have a better understanding of why it sees any threats as battles, and is therefore driven to defend you. While the outcome was not always favorable, its commitment to your wellbeing was solid. Now take five minutes, and do a life review from your new perspective. See your defiant ego-self committing to your safety throughout your lifetime, and thank it for its righteous intentions. While the choices often have created greater unrest and more challenging battles, the intention was pure.

Witnessing all aspects of your "self" in a non-judgmental way is key to finding and maintaining better peace of mind. Now that you have a better understanding of the reasoning behind your ego's initiatives, you are ready to begin strategizing on how to create greater peace in your life, starting from the inside out!

I.

Laying Plans

1. Sun Tzu said: The art of war is of vital importance to the State.

2. It is a matter of life and death, a road either to safety or to ruin. Hence it is a subject of inquiry which can on no account be neglected.

3. The art of war, then, is governed by five constant factors, to be taken into account in one's deliberations, when seeking to determine the conditions obtaining in the field.

4. These are:
   (1) The Moral Law;
   (2) Heaven;
   (3) Earth;
   (4) The Commander;
   (5) Method and discipline.

5,6. The Moral Law causes the people to be in complete accord with their ruler, so that they will follow him regardless of their lives, undismayed by any danger.

7. Heaven signifies night and day, cold and heat, times and seasons.

8. Earth comprises distances, great and small; danger and security; open ground and narrow passes; the chances of life and death.

9. The Commander stands for the virtues of wisdom, sincerely, benevolence, courage and strictness.

10. By method and discipline are to be understood the marshaling of the army in its proper subdivisions, the graduations of rank among the officers, the maintenance of roads by which supplies may reach the army, and the control of military expenditure.

11. These five heads should be familiar to every general: he who knows them will be victorious; he who knows them not will fail.

12. Therefore, in your deliberations, when seeking to determine the military conditions, let them be made the basis of a comparison, in this wise:

13. (1) Which of the two sovereigns is imbued with the Moral law?

(2) Which of the two generals has most ability?

(3) With whom lie the advantages derived from Heaven and Earth?

(4) On which side is discipline most rigorously enforced?

(5) Which army is stronger?

(6) On which side are officers and men more highly trained?

(7) In which army is there the greater constancy both in reward and punishment?

14. By means of these seven considerations I can forecast victory or defeat.

15. The general that hearkens to my counsel and acts upon it, will conquer: let such a one be retained in command! The general that hearkens not to my counsel nor acts upon it, will suffer defeat: let such a one be dismissed!

16. While heading the profit of my counsel, avail yourself also of any helpful circumstances over and beyond the ordinary rules.

17. According as circumstances are favorable, one should modify one's plans.

18. All warfare is based on deception.

19. Hence, when able to attack, we must seem unable; when using our forces, we must seem inactive; when

we are near, we must make the enemy believe we are far away; when far away, we must make him believe we are near.

20. Hold out baits to entice the enemy. Feign disorder, and crush him.

21. If he is secure at all points, be prepared for him. If he is in superior strength, evade him.

22. If your opponent is of choleric temper, seek to irritate him. Pretend to be weak, that he may grow arrogant.

23. If he is taking his ease, give him no rest. If his forces are united, separate them.

24. Attack him where he is unprepared, appear where you are not expected.

25. These military devices, leading to victory, must not be divulged beforehand.

26. Now the general who wins a battle makes many calculations in his temple ere the battle is fought. The general who loses a battle makes but few calculations beforehand. Thus do many calculations lead to victory, and few calculations to defeat: how much more no calculation at all! It is by attention to this point that I can foresee who is likely to win or lose.

I. Laying Plans

Before venturing out into any major endeavor, it is important that you have a plan of attack. To make vast changes in your life without doing the preparatory work, will ensure a fast and ruthless defeat. In this chapter, Sun Tzu lays the groundwork that you need to adhere to when setting out to wage a war against your inner turmoil.

*NOTE: Any text from THE ART OF WAR that is referenced in the Study Guide segments below will be italicized.

1. In #1, Sun Tzu opened *The Art of War* saying, *"The are of war is of vital importance to the state."* Why do you think you were drawn to this book and manual at this time in your life?

2. #2 states, *"It is a matter of life and death, a road to safety or ruin. Therefore it is a subject that must be thoroughly studied."* Do you have a sense of urgency around creating an inner sense of peace? Why or why not?

3. How might your life be *"ruined"* if you continue living it with the inner turmoil you experience?

4. What would safety look like to you now? Make a list of the elements that would contribute to feeling safe in your life.

5. Could the safety potentially come from changing your perception about feeling safe? What if you didn't need anything from the list above in order to feel safe? Do you think you would experience greater peace?

6. In #3, Sun Tzu lists five factors that govern the art of war as being:
   1) The Moral Law,
   2) Heaven,
   3) Earth,
   4) The Commander, and
   5) Method and Discipline. #5, 6:

The Moral Law causes people to be in complete accord with their ruler and to follow him regardless of any danger to their lives." Are you in complete accord with yourself? If not, list any areas where you currently struggle to trust your own innate wisdom.

7. #7: *"Heaven signifies night and day, cold and heat, times and seasons."* These are all environmental factors that have an impact on your sense of security and peace. Do you feel at one with the world around you? Do you feel supported, or do you often feel at odds with factors like time? On a scale from one to ten, rate how environmentally supported you currently feel in your life (1 being "barely at all" and 10 being "extremely supported"):

1——2——3——4——5——6——7——8——9——10

8. #8: *"Earth comprises near and far distances, dangerous and secure positions; open ground and narrow passes; the chances of life and death."* In what areas of your life do you believe your well-being is being threatened most? In your work relationships? Debts? Personal relationships? Faith? Or other?

9. #9: *"The Commander stands for virtues of wisdom, sincerity, benevolence, courage and strictness."* Do a personal inventory. Which of these virtues do you possess? Which of these traits would you like to cultivate further within yourself?

10. #10: *"Method and Discipline describes the disposition of the army, its subdivisions, the gradation and deployment of its officers, the maintenance of roads that carry supplies to the army, and the management of military expenditure."* While we will seek out methods that you can deploy in your battle to find peace of mind, you need to have discipline to do so. On a scale from one to ten, rate how much discipline you currently have in your commitment to make inner peace with the warring factions in your mind (1 being "very little" and 10 being "a great deal"):

1———2———3———4———5———6———7———8———9———10

11. Sun Tzu states, *"the general who knows the five factors will be victorious."* Do an inventory of your two armies. Respond to each of the questions below to determine which aspect of yourself (your higher-self or your ego-self) has advantage:

    Which of the two sovereigns is imbued with the Moral law?

    Which of the two generals has most ability?

    With whom lie the advantages derived from Heaven and Earth?

    On which side is discipline most rigorously enforced?

    Which army is stronger?

    On which side are officers and men more highly trained?

    In which army is there the greater constancy both in reward and punishment?

12. Based on the inventory you did above, what currently has the greatest command of your mind—your ego or higher self?

13. Sun Tzu suggested that you *"avail yourself also to any helpful circumstances that give you advantages beyond ordinary conditions."* Is there anything or anyone in your life that might further support you in finding greater peace of mind? For example, do you have a friend or family member who demonstrates compassion and deeper understanding that you could share your discoveries and insights with, as you delve into this treatise? If so, ask if you can share your growth experience with them?

14. #18.*"All warfare is based on deception. #19. Hence, when able to attack, seem as if unable to attack; when using forces actively, seem inactive; when nearby, make the energy believe you are far away; when far away, make the enemy believe you are nearby."* In it's attempt to assert itself, what ways do your ego deceive your? Make is list of the misguided beliefs that you have perpetuated about yourself and others.

15. #20, *"Hold out baits to entice the enemy to act. Feign disorder, and strike him when he seeks to take advantage."* How do you think your inner critic takes advantage of you? For example, does it keep you feeling "Not good enough" thus you don't take action on manifesting your desires? Does it sabotage you when you are doing well? Make a list of the ways that it seeks to take advantage of you.

16. #21: *If your enemy is secure at all points, prepare for his attack. If he has superior strength, evade him."* How might you evade your ego as it attacks your peace of mind? Write three things you could do that might disempower that critical voice in your head.

17. #22: *"If your enemy bares a short temper, seek to irritate him. Pretend to be weak, so he becomes arrogant."* Take note when you find yourself short-tempered with others. Usually if someone's behavior irritates you, your judgment of him or her reflects your own judgment of yourself. You might say, *"Wait a second. I don't behave in that way. In fact, I am the exact opposite."* Very often, you may have previously judged the behavior in yourself, and in response, you have erased it from your behaviors. In fact, very often you behave in the exact opposite way. For example, I react harshly to others being late. Based on this model, I would conclude that my strong reaction against latecomers if not about me, because I am almost always on time. In fact, I'm usually very early. If you investigate further, you may discover that your intolerance of latecomers is extreme because you wouldn't dare let yourself be late. Ultimately, you resent others behaving in the way because you no longer tolerate in yourself. Note: This does not mean that the behavior is acceptable. Being late for no good reason is rude. However, if your reaction to that behavior or any other is very judgment and harsh, you may need to look deeper within for your own intolerance of anything short of perfection in yourself.

18. #23: *"If your enemy takes his ease, give him no rest. If his forces unite, separate them."* In this case, you are encouraged to be unrelenting when dealing with the enemy. On a scale from one to ten, rate how much you wish to make peace with your inner critic (1 being "not at all" and 10 being "very much so"):

1——2——3——4——5——6——7——8——9——10

19. **#24:** *Attack your enemy where he is unprepared, appear where he does not expect you."* Your ego does not expect you to befriend it. It is always on the defense, awaiting attack. By befriending it, you will "appear where he does not expect you." List three actions you can take to befriend your ego, then be sure to take them.

20. **#25:** *"These military deceptions that bring victory must not be revealed as deceptions before they succeed."* This tenet suggests secrecy; not revealing your strategies. Note that there are two different theories in response to discussing self-improvement goals and strategies. Some suggest that speaking about them actually weakens them—the energy is not as focused as it might have been when you are commanding it within. Others suggest that sharing your goals and strategies sets accountability in motion and actually can further strengthen your drive and conviction. You are your own expert, so in this case, you should decide what works best for you. Write about your position on this matter, and follow your own inner guidance on whether to share your plan with others or to keep it to yourself.

21. **#26:** *"Now the general who wins a battle makes many calculations in his headquarters before he fights a battle . . . many calculations lead to victory . . ."* This tenet emphasizes the power of careful strategic planning. Do you tend to be a planner? If so, does it help you to move forward in your life, or is it a way to further avoid taking action? Where does planning fit into your present initiative in this battle to find peace?

II.

Waging War

1. Sun Tzu said: In the operations of war, where there are in the field a thousand swift chariots, as many heavy chariots, and a hundred thousand mail-clad soldiers, with provisions enough to carry them a thousand li, the expenditure at home and at the front, including entertainment of guests, small items such as glue and paint, and sums spent on chariots and armor, will reach the total of a thousand ounces of silver per day. Such is the cost of raising an army of 100,000 men.

2. When you engage in actual fighting, if victory is long in coming, then men's weapons will grow dull and their ardor will be damped. If you lay siege to a town, you will exhaust your strength.

3. Again, if the campaign is protracted, the resources of the State will not be equal to the strain.

4. Now, when your weapons are dulled, your ardor damped, your strength exhausted and your treasure spent, other chieftains will spring up to take advantage of your extremity. Then no man, however wise, will be able to avert the consequences that must ensue.

5. Thus, though we have heard of stupid haste in war, cleverness has never been seen associated with long delays.

6. There is no instance of a country having benefited from prolonged warfare.

7. It is only one who is thoroughly acquainted with the evils of war that can thoroughly understand the profitable way of carrying it on.

8. The skillful soldier does not raise a second levy, neither are his supply-wagons loaded more than twice.

9. Bring war material with you from home, but forage on the enemy. Thus the army will have food enough for its needs.

10. Poverty of the State exchequer causes an army to be maintained by contributions from a distance. Contributing to maintain an army at a distance causes the people to be impoverished.

11. On the other hand, the proximity of an army causes prices to go up; and high prices cause the people's substance to be drained away.

12. When their substance is drained away, the peasantry will be afflicted by heavy exactions.

13,14. With this loss of substance and exhaustion of strength, the homes of the people will be stripped bare, and three-tenths of their income will be dissipated; while government expenses for broken chariots, worn-out horses, breast-plates and helmets, bows and arrows, spears and shields, protective mantles, draught-oxen and heavy wagons, will amount to four-tenths of its total revenue.

15. Hence a wise general makes a point of foraging on the enemy. One cartload of the enemy's provisions is equivalent to twenty of one's own, and likewise a single picul of his provender is equivalent to twenty from one's own store.

16. Now in order to kill the enemy, our men must be roused to anger; that there may be advantage from defeating the enemy, they must have their rewards.

17. Therefore in chariot fighting, when ten or more chariots have been taken, those should be rewarded who took the first. Our own flags should be substituted for those of the enemy, and the chariots

mingled and used in conjunction with ours. The captured soldiers should be kindly treated and kept.

18. This is called, using the conquered foe to augment one's own strength.

19. In war, then, let your great object be victory, not lengthy campaigns.

20. Thus it may be known that the leader of armies is the arbiter of the people's fate, the man on whom it depends whether the nation shall be in peace or in peril.

II. *Waging War*

In this segment of the treatise, Sun Tzu discusses the costs of waging a war. These costs not only reference potential monetary losses, but tactical and energetic as well.

1. #1: In this section of his text, Sun Tzu lays out the costs to waging a war, stating that it would cost a thousand ounces of silver each day to raise an army of 100,000 men. He breaks down the expenses and then provides an overview of them. Write two columns on a piece of paper. Title the first column "Cost to Wage War" and title the second column, "Cost *Not* to Wage a War". Then in each column make a list of what it would cost you to wage this war against your ego? In the second column, list what it would cost you not to do this emotional work on yourself. Again, "costs" reach far beyond monetary. What emotional, intellectual, physical and spiritual challenges will you continue to face if you don't find a greater sense of inner peace?

2. #2: *"When you engage the enemy in actual fighting, if victory takes a long time to achieve, then your men's weapons will dull and their enthusiasm for the fight will diminish. If you lay siege to a town, you will exhaust your strength. #3: "If the campaign is protracted, the resources of the State will not bear the strain."* In these statements Sun Tzu discourages actual fighting, especially of any length. What is

important here as you strategize with gaining insights and clarity around the workings of your ego, is that you set specific goals and don't prolong your battle. It is said that it takes 28 days to change a habit. Would you be willing to focus on healing your judgmental thoughts and making peace with your ego for the next 28 days?

3. In #4, Sun Tzu cautions that *"not even your wisest council will be able to prevent the resulting consequences"* when your condition is severely weakened. Write a list of the ways in which the reign of your ego has negatively affected your life. How has it diminished your energy, and opportunities?

4. #5: *"Thus, though we have heard of foolishly rushing to war, we have never seen cleverness in war allocated with long delays."* Very often when we are struggling with changing a particular habit or behavior, we procrastinate. We often busy ourselves with other things to avoid dealing with issues. How have you been delaying your battle with your ego? What excuses or "busy activities" have you been pursuing to avoid dealing with this issue?

5. #6: *"No country has ever benefitted from a prolong war."* In the self-help world, one can get lost on doing a great deal of reflection without completing a course of action for an issue. It is helpful to commit to a particular length of time that you would chose to work on this issue, with the knowing that you can then move forward in your life. What is the target date that you would like to apply to this task?

6. #7: *"Only one familiar with the evils of war can thoroughly know the best way to fight it."* How much knowledge do you have of your inner workings? Are you aware of the times when your criticism rears itself? Are you able to put out of your ego, and witness your behavior? If you haven't

yet been able to do so, try to cultivate your "witness self." This is a part of you who can watch your ego in action. Often the practice of meditation helps you to cultivate the witness. Being able to witness your ego in action allows you to associate your identity less with it, so that you can see it as only a part of your personality. This in turn helps you identify less with it, so that you are able to become less defensive when you find your ego acting out in ways that do not serve you. Practice cultivating your witness-self, and write about any insights you gain in doing so.

7. #8: In this segment, Sun Tzu states that you should not raise a second levy, or load supply wagons more than twice. In the world of self-help, you can become addicted to reading, researching or experimenting more and more, as another way of avoiding taking action. If you fully commit to healing yourself, you stop obsessively reading the books and doing the research, and focus on moving forward. Do you have a tendency to over-research and under-act? Explain.

8. #9: Sun Tzu suggests that you *"forage on the enemy for additional supplies,"* so that you will have enough of your own food to survive. In other words, you should take as much as you can from the supplies of the enemy, so that you do not run short of your own. As previously mentioned, your ego-self is well-intended, and it has served you in the past. If it had not, you would not have followed its leads. What sustenance has your ego brought to you thus far in your life? Write a list of how your critical self has served you until now.

9. #10: *"Contributing to a distant army impoverishes the state treasury. Contributing to maintain an army at a distance in turn causes the people to be impoverished."* This

statement is a tricky one to decipher. Whether the people or the state, contributing at a distance wears down the funds. Relating this to your own personal journey of development, you need to become intimate with your ego. Keeping it at a distance depletes your energy and obscures your vision. How have you been protecting yourself by keeping your ego at a distance? Have you blamed others for your shortcomings? Have you worn a mask of acceptance of others, while seething inside with resentment? Do you trivialize the way it has hurt you and others? List ways in which you have kept your ego at a distance?

10. #11, #12, #13 & #14. Sun Tzu states that an army nearby *"causes prices to go up and provisions to be depleted,"* stealing from the people's ability to sustain themselves, and subsequently making the government extract more from them. Poverty abounds. Thus, translated to your own healing journey, being too obsessed with your shortcomings can also impoverish your spirit. Just as you can become obsessive in avoiding dealing with your problems, you can also become so obsessed with the issues, that you become hopeless and depressed. Have you felt hopeless about healing your critical mind? Explain.

11. #15: *"So a wise general forages on the enemy instead of his own people. One cartload of an enemy's provisions equals twenty of one's own, and likewise a single ration of food is equivalent to twenty from one's own stores."* In this tactic, Sun Tzu encourages you to nourish your army with the enemy's provisions. If we see the ego's provisions as being that which sustains it, we know that its root is fear. While one might suggest that taking away the fear will feed your highest self, but this is not the case. Fear will always exist. While many of us are misguided, believing that our fears need to be annihilated, the trick is

to take action in your life despite the fear. You will waste a great deal of time and energy attempting to rid yourself of your fears. Forge ahead while noting the fears. Knowledge is power, so write a list of the fears that you believe are keeping you from moving forward in your life.

12. #16/17: *"In order to kill the enemy, the men must be spurred into fighting rage that they may find advantage from defeating the enemy, they must also receive a personal reward . . . in chariot fighting, when ten or more chariots have been taken, reward those who took the first."* In both these tenets Sun Tzu encourages rewarding outstanding members of your army. Do you acknowledge yourself when you work through your fears? If so, how? If not, write three steps you can take towards rewarding yourself in future.

13. #18: *". . . Treat captured soldiers well and provide for them . . . This is called, using the conquered foe to augment your strength."* In this strategy, the author suggests that you provide for your captured soldiers. Again, this supports the ideology that to treat your ego-self badly serves no purpose. In fact, it weakens your position against it. For example, to criticize the critical aspect of yourself perpetuates the negative cycle of self-loathing. It is important that you accept all aspects of yourself, including those aspects that you do not like. What character trait that you possess upsets you the most? What steps can you take to honoring and accepting that trait?

14. #19: *"So in war, let a victory be your main objective, not the conduct of lengthy and costly campaigns."* In this case, Sun Tzu encourages you to focus on your main objective. For the sake of clarity, in one sentence write out what specifically your main objective is.

15. #20: *"Thus the military leadership determines the peo-ple's fate, and the man who commands the military determines whether the nation shall see peace or peril,"* In this phrase, you are reminded that you are in control of situations. When you find yourself reacting to others and feeling out of control, take a deep breathe before responding, or even leave the situation. This will assist you in maintaining your control. Try this and write about your experience.

III.

Attack By Stratagem

1. Sun Tzu said: In the practical art of war, the best thing of all is to take the enemy's country whole and intact; to shatter and destroy it is not so good. So, too, it is better to recapture an army entire than to destroy it, to capture a regiment, a detachment or a company entire than to destroy them.

2. Hence to fight and conquer in all your battles is not supreme excellence; supreme excellence consists in breaking the enemy's resistance without fighting.

3. Thus the highest form of generalship is to balk the enemy's plans; the next best is to prevent the junction of the enemy's forces; the next in order is to attack the enemy's army in the field; and the worst policy of all is to besiege walled cities.

4. The rule is, not to besiege walled cities if it can possibly be avoided. The preparation of mantlets, movable shelters, and various implements of war, will take up three whole months; and the piling up of mounds over against the walls will take three months more.

5. The general, unable to control his irritation, will launch his men to the assault like swarming ants, with the result that one-third of his men are slain, while the town still remains untaken. Such are the disastrous effects of a siege.

6. Therefore the skillful leader subdues the enemy's troops without any fighting; he captures their cities without laying siege to them; he overthrows their kingdom without lengthy operations in the field.

7. With his forces intact he will dispute the mastery of the Empire, and thus, without losing a man, his triumph will be complete. This is the method of attacking by stratagem.

8. It is the rule in war, if our forces are ten to the enemy's one, to surround him; if five to one, to attack him; if twice as numerous, to divide our army into two.

9. If equally matched, we can offer battle; if slightly inferior in numbers, we can avoid the enemy; f quite unequal in every way, we can flee from him.

10. Hence, though an obstinate fight may be made by a small force, in the end it must be captured by the larger force.

11. Now the general is the bulwark of the State; if the bulwark is complete at all points; the State will be strong; if the bulwark is defective, the State will be weak.

12. There are three ways in which a ruler can bring misfortune upon his army:

13. (1) By commanding the army to advance or to retreat, being ignorant of the fact that it cannot obey. This is called hobbling the army.

14. (2) By attempting to govern an army in the same way as he administers a kingdom, being ignorant of the conditions which obtain in an army. This causes restlessness in the soldier's minds.

15. (3) By employing the officers of his army without discrimination, through ignorance of the military principle of adaptation to circumstances. This shakes the confidence of the soldiers.

16. But when the army is restless and distrustful, trouble is sure to come from the other feudal princes. This is simply bringing anarchy into the army, and flinging victory away.

17. Thus we may know that there are five essentials for victory:

   (1) He will win who knows when to fight and when not to fight.

   (2) He will win who knows how to handle both superior and inferior forces.

   (3) He will win whose army is animated by the same spirit throughout all its ranks.

   (4) He will win who, prepared himself, waits to take the enemy unprepared.

   (5) He will win who has military capacity and is not interfered with by the sovereign.

18. Hence the saying: If you know the enemy and know yourself, you need not fear the result of a hundred battles. If you know yourself but not the enemy, for every victory gained you will also suffer a defeat. If you know neither the enemy nor yourself, you will succumb in every battle.

III. *Attack By Stratagem*

In this segment of the treatise, Sue Tzu shares insights on basic stratagem necessary to put you in a power position with your ego opponent. Note that he opens by saying that supreme excellence is breaking the enemy down without fighting.

1. #1: *"Sun Tzu said: In the practical art of war, the best thing of all is to take the enemy's country whole and intact; to shatter and destroy it is not so good. So, too, it is better to recapture an army entire than to destroy it, to capture a regiment, a detachment or a company entire than to destroy them."* This tenet reflects our earlier insight that the ego and its many voices are not to be annihilated, but noted, heard, and understood. Once you are able to witness the ego in action, and not identify yourself with it, you can then move beyond it. For example, jealousy. At times you may find yourself being jealous. Your first reaction may be to judge the jealousy as wrong and bad. If, however, you step back and witness the jealousy, noting where it has come from, and having compassion for that part of you that doesn't feel good enough, you can work on honoring and appreciating yourself more. This, in turn, does not destroy the ego, but gives it less power over you. Think of an individual whom you feel jealousy towards. Note how you feel about being jealous. Then write a compassionate letter to that jealous voice in your head. Then think of a step you can take to feel better about yourself. Note how you feel after taking these steps.

2. #2: *"Hence to fight and conquer in all your battles is not supreme excellence; supreme excellence consists in breaking the enemy's resistance without fighting."* This principle reflects the futility and loss of energy when you constantly attempt to battle against the parts of yourself that you struggle with. You can break your ego's resistance simply by pulling yourself from identifying with it by witnessing it in action, and by choosing compassion over judgment of it. Try this next time you find yourself procrastinating. Note that you are doing so, have compassion for that aspect of your personality, then move through it. Try this, and note any shifts that occur in your experience.

3. #3: *"Thus the highest form of generalship is to balk the enemy's plans; the next best is to prevent the junction of the enemy's forces; the next in order is to attack the enemy's army in the field; and the worst policy of all is to besiege walled cities."* In this strategy the author provides you with an order to priority for your plan of attack. In the beginning he suggests you draw back—maneuver yourself so that the enemy cannot follow through with their plans. Secondly get in the way of the enemy armies joining forces. Thirdly attack in the field and lastly, the worst policy is to attack the walled cities. Translating this to your internal battle, your best plan of attack then would be divert your ego from its original plans. In order to accomplish this, you must have an idea of what its strategy is. For example, you know that jealousy is an issue for you. A friend announces that they got a raise and a promotion. Ideally if you know that your ego tends to gossip and bad mouth others when feeling jealous, take five minutes each day to take some deep breaths. Focus on what you are proud of within yourself. Talk to your ego, ensuring it that you have compassion for it, and then when you see

yourself tempted to speak ill of the individual, stop yourself from doing so. Try this, and write about your findings.

4. **#4:** *"The rule is, not to besiege walled cities if it can possibly be avoided. The preparation of mantlets, movable shelters, and various implements of war, will take up three whole months; and the piling up of mounds over against the walls will take three months more."* In this tenet, Sun Tzu further discourages attacking walled cities, referencing the time it would take to do so. If we parallel attacking a walled city with trying to attack the ego, the walled cities would reference where the ego is most defensive, and expecting attack. There is an old saying, "If you build a fortress, the armies will come." In the case of the ego, the more unwilling you are to face the ego squarely, honor, acknowledge and move beyond it, the larger the defensive walls will be built. Write a list of the areas in your life where you get defensive. To assist you in locating your defenses, you will note that whenever someone references an aspect of your personality, where you defiantly fight back and defend your position, is most often areas where you do not want to face your own perceived weaknesses.

5. **#5:** *"The general, unable to control his irritation, will launch his men to the assault like swarming ants, with the result that one-third of his men are slain, while the town still remains untaken. Such are the disastrous effects of a siege."* In this case, your ego is the irritated commander and general. The more you lack patience and continue to judge yourself harshly, the greater you lose. Write a list of the ways in which you are most impatient with yourself and others. Then sit for five minutes and honor yourself for having the courage and steadfastness to face your impatience, knowing that you are aware and will continue to work on it.

6. **#6:** *"Therefore the skillful leader subdues the enemy's troops without any fighting; he captures their cities without laying siege to them; he overthrows their kingdom without lengthy operations in the field."* In this case, the skillful leader is fast in his actions and non-reactive; he does not fight the enemy, but subdues them. What small action step might you take to subdue one of the faces of your ego (faces being impatience, jealousy, anger, hatred, self-contempt, alienation, criticism of others, anxiousness, passive aggressive behavior, etc.?

7. **#7:** *"With his forces intact he will dispute the mastery of the Empire, and thus, without losing a man, his triumph will be complete. This is the method of attacking by stratagem."* Again, the winner has a strategy and is non-reactive. Another way to become less reactive when your ego rears its head is to witness it in action, seeing it as separate from yourself. When you may behave in a way that is governed by your ego, you are not the ego. It is an anxious part of yourself that is struggling to survive. Next time you note your ego at war, take a moment to witness it in action, as if you were watching a movie. Then have a dialogue with it. Ask it what it is saying that you need to hear. Tell it that it is safe and that you understand its reason, however ineffective its actions are. Listen to its reasoning and write about your findings.

8. **#8:** *"It is the rule in war, if our forces are ten to the enemy's one, to surround him; if five to one, to attack him; if twice as numerous, to divide our army into two."* **#9:** *"If equally matched, we can offer battle; if slightly inferior in numbers, we can avoid the enemy; if quite unequal in every way, we can flee from him."* **#10:** *"Hence, though an obstinate fight may be made by a small force, in the end it must be captured by the larger force."* These three tactical suggestions

relate to your strength as an army. Is your commitment "ten to the enemy's one" or are you ready to flee from the stronger enemy? Now that you've done some work on this inner battle, on a scale from one to ten (one being "barely committed" and ten being "very committed", again rate how strong your commitment is to beating your ego's drives. Has your commitment strengthened or weakened?

1———2———3———4———5———6———7———8———9———10

9. #11: *"Now the general is the bulwark of the State; if the bulwark is complete at all points; the State will be strong; if the bulwark is defective, the State will be weak."* The general in your battle with your ego would be that part of your that aches for peace, growth and well being. Do you see your inner general "complete at all points" or is he wavering in his commitment and strategies? If so, identify where he is weak.

10. #12-#15: *"There are three ways in which a ruler can bring misfortune upon his army: (1) By commanding the army to advance or to retreat, being ignorant of the fact that it cannot obey. This is called hobbling the army. (2) By attempting to govern an army in the same way as he administers a kingdom, being ignorant of the conditions which obtain in an army. This causes restlessness in the soldier's minds. (3) By employing the officers of his army without discrimination, through ignorance of the military principle of adaptation to circumstances. This shakes the confidence of the soldiers."* Wisdom and the ability to adapt are highlighted in these tenets. Do you find yourself to be rigid in your ways, or do you easily adapt when thrown curve balls? On a scale from one to ten (one being "very little" and ten being "very much so", rate how adaptable you believe you are.

1———2———3———4———5———6———7———8———9———10

11. *#16: "But when the army is restless and distrustful, trouble is sure to come from the other feudal princes. This is simply bringing anarchy into the army, and flinging victory away."* As you fight your internal battle, do you find others are pulled into your toxic energy? This is very often the case. If so, provide examples.

#17: Thus we may know that there are five essentials for victory:

    (1) He will win who knows when to fight and when not to fight.

    (2) He will win who knows how to handle both superior and inferior forces.

    (3) He will win whose army is animated by the same spirit throughout all its ranks.

    (4) He will win who, prepared himself, waits to take the enemy unprepared.

    (5) He will win who has military capacity and is not interfered with by the sovereign."

You could see this list of essentials as being

    1) learning to step away and be non-reactive,

    2) Knowing yourself inside and out (your strengths and weaknesses),

    3) having passion for growth on all levels,

    4) being prepared and finding tools and strategies, and

    5) not allowing others to sway your inner knowing. It is important to know how strong your army is. On a scale from one to ten (one being "very little" and ten being "very much"), rate yourself in each of these areas:

1) Learning to step away and be non-reactive

1——2——3——4——5——6——7——8——9——10

2) Knowing yourself inside and out (your strengths and weaknesses):

1———2———3———4———5———6———7———8———9———10

3) Having passion for growth on all levels:

1———2———3———4———5———6———7———8———9———10

4) Being prepared and finding tools and strategies:

1———2———3———4———5———6———7———8———9———10

5) Not allowing others to sway your inner knowing:

1———2———3———4———5———6———7———8———9———10

12. #18: *"Hence the saying: If you know the enemy and know yourself, you need not fear the result of a hundred battles. If you know yourself but not the enemy, for every victory gained you will also suffer a defeat. If you know neither the enemy nor yourself, you will succumb in every battle."* In other words, when dealing with your own inner battle towards inner peace and joy, you must be brutally honest and fully transparent with yourself. While you must find compassion, you must also be honest about your shortcomings and find the willingness to face them head on and work on them. Write a short paragraph or two about the self-honesty and transparency you possess. Honor your strength and speak truthfully of your weaknesses.

IV.

Tactical Dispositions

1. Sun Tzu said: The good fighters of old first put themselves beyond the possibility of defeat, and then waited for an opportunity of defeating the enemy.

2. To secure ourselves against defeat lies in our own hands, but the opportunity of defeating the enemy is provided by the enemy himself.

3. Thus the good fighter is able to secure himself against defeat, but cannot make certain of defeating the enemy.

4. Hence the saying: One may know how to conquer without being able to do it.

5. Security against defeat implies defensive tactics; ability to defeat the enemy means taking the offensive.

6. Standing on the defensive indicates insufficient strength; attacking, a superabundance of strength.

7. The general who is skilled in defense hides in the most secret recesses of the earth; he who is skilled in attack flashes forth from the topmost heights of heaven. Thus on the one hand we have ability to protect ourselves; on the other, a victory that is complete.

8. To see victory only when it is within the ken of the common herd is not the acme of excellence.

9. Neither is it the acme of excellence if you fight and conquer and the whole Empire says, "Well done!"

10. To lift an autumn hair is no sign of great strength; to see the sun and moon is no sign of sharp sight; to hear the noise of thunder is no sign of a quick ear.

11. What the ancients called a clever fighter is one who not only wins, but excels in winning with ease.

12. Hence his victories bring him neither reputation for wisdom nor credit for courage.

13. He wins his battles by making no mistakes. Making no mistakes is what establishes the certainty of victory, for it means conquering an enemy that is already defeated.

14. Hence the skillful fighter puts himself into a position which makes defeat impossible, and does not miss the moment for defeating the enemy.

15. Thus it is that in war the victorious strategist only seeks battle after the victory has been won, whereas he who is destined to defeat first fights and afterwards looks for victory.

16. The consummate leader cultivates the moral law, and strictly adheres to method and discipline; thus it is in his power to control success.

17. In respect of military method, we have, firstly, Measurement; secondly, Estimation of quantity; thirdly, Calculation; fourthly, Balancing of chances; fifthly, Victory.

18. Measurement owes its existence to Earth; Estimation of quantity to Measurement; Calculation to Estimation of quantity; Balancing of chances to Calculation; and Victory to Balancing of chances.

19. A victorious army opposed to a routed one, is as a pound's weight placed in the scale against a single grain.

20. The onrush of a conquering force is like the bursting of pent-up waters into a chasm a thousand fathoms deep.

STUDY GUIDE

IV. Tactical Dispositions

In this chapter Sun Tzu shares insights on specific tactical positions. He emphasizes that the most powerful thing to do is wait and allow the enemy to put themselves in an inferior position. Thus with patience, keen observation and solid strategy, your ego will likely put itself into a position of defeat.

1. #1: *"Sun Tzu said: The good fighters of old first put themselves beyond the possibility of defeat, and then waited for an opportunity of defeating the enemy."* To put yourself "beyond the possibility of defeat" you must envision yourself winning the battle with your ego. Take five to ten minutes and close your eyes. Image a perfect day— one in which you are experiencing great joy and peace of mind. There are no inner negative voices to battle, no outer reflections of inner turmoil. You experience ease, joy and laughter. All of your desires are being manifest. Feel into your perfect day with all of your senses, and imagine it happening now. Once you have completed this exercise, write about your experience.

2. #2: *"To secure ourselves against defeat lies in our own hands, but the opportunity of defeating the enemy is provided by the enemy himself."* #3: *"Thus the good fighter is able to secure himself against defeat, but cannot make certain of defeating the enemy."* Your ego provides you with plenty of opportunities to defeat it. Again, defeating

it starts with having compassion for it. If you judge it, you are perpetuating the negative thought cycle. Next time you note your ego in reaction mode, stop. Speak to it, and comfort it. Thank it for its misguided choices, forgive yourself and then move on. Try focusing on this practice for at least a week. Write about any discoveries you have after doing so.

3. #4: *"Hence the saying: One may know how to conquer without being able to do it."* You have an innate wisdom within you. When you connect to your higher self, that "knowing" speaks to you. How much do you trust your inner knowing? On a scale from one to ten (one being "very little" and ten being "very much so", rate how much you trust your inner knowing.

1——2——3——4——5——6——7——8——9——10

4. #5: *"Security against defeat implies defensive tactics; ability to defeat the enemy means taking the offensive."* You are taking the offensive by doing these exercises. You will know when you take a defensive stance, because when you do so, you feel like a victim. Next time you feel like a victim in a situation, stop and reflect on what part you played in the drama. How were you being self-destructive? How did the situation serve you? Practice this exercise each time you catch yourself feeling like a victim of individuals or circumstances. Write about your findings.

5. #6: *"Standing on the defensive indicates insufficient strength; attacking, a superabundance of strength. #7: The general who is skilled in defense hides in the most secret recesses of the earth; he who is skilled in attack flashes forth from the topmost heights of heaven. Thus on the one hand we have ability to protect ourselves; on the*

other, a victory that is complete." Hiding from your ego, or pretending it does not exist protects you from dealing with it, but makes your life miserable. Dealing with it offers "complete victory." Write a list of ways in which you would experience victory in your battle with your ego. Then go through the list. Are you experiencing anything you listed now, even to a small degree? If so, note it and understand that focusing on the good that is coming your way will increase it.

6. *#8: "To see victory only when it is within the ken of the common herd is not the acme of excellence."* Doing your emotional work does not necessarily follow the status quo. You will likely stand out from the "common herd". At times you may experience resistance and even criticism from your peers. This can be challenging. When you are criticized, write down the criticism, and then write a response from your higher wisdom of knowing. Doing this will increase your strength and perseverance when criticism rears its destructive army against you.

7. *#9: "Neither is it the acme of excellence if you fight and conquer and the whole Empire says, 'Well done!'"* Looking for accolades and reassurance from others can also be a trap that your masterful ego plays. While it may feed your ego, you need to gather credit and support from within yourself. Write a "Well done!" list for yourself, honoring what you are currently doing in your life that you are proud of.

8. *#10: "To lift an autumn hair is no sign of great strength; to see the sun and moon is no sign of sharp sight; to hear the noise of thunder is no sign of a quick ear."* To respond to the mundane daily occurrences as they arise will not bring you deeper joy. However, being in the present moment, seeing, hearing, experiencing, and appreciating

nature is a gift and can raise your energy so that you are stronger in your battle with your ego. Take a 15-minute walk in nature, focusing on its magic. Then if you are inspired, write about your experience,

9. *#11: "What the ancients called a clever fighter is one who not only wins, but excels in winning with ease."* Ease is the key word here. While your initial experience in this battle may be difficult, you will find that in time, the more compassion you give yourself, the more you will experience greater ease. What would greater ease in your life look like? Write about it.

10. *#12: "Hence his victories bring him neither reputation for wisdom nor credit for courage. #13 "He wins his battles by making no mistakes. Making no mistakes is what establishes the certainty of victory, for it means conquering an enemy that is already defeated. #14: "Hence the skillful fighter puts himself into a position which makes defeat impossible, and does not miss the moment for defeating the enemy."* In this case, "making no mistakes" could be interpreted as being ruthless in your commitment to finding peace. What are you willing to forego in order to win this war? Write a list.

11. *#15: "Thus it is that in war the victorious strategist only seeks battle after the victory has been won, whereas he who is destined to defeat first fights and afterwards looks for victory."* This tenet deals with the focus is for a victorious opponent. The commander who focuses solely on defeat and only afterwards looks for victory does not pre-empt but puts all of her energy into the task at hand. Do you have a tendency to stay busy and unfocused as a means to avoiding dealing with issues when they arise? If so, describe what tactics you use.

12. *#16: "The consummate leader cultivates the moral law, and strictly adheres to method and discipline; thus it is in his power to control success."* The consummate leader controls his success through method and discipline. You are provided with method in this text. Do you ever lack discipline? If so, what action steps can you take to cultivate greater discipline with the emotional growth work that you are doing?

13. *#17: "In respect of military method, we have, firstly, Measurement; secondly, Estimation of quantity; thirdly, Calculation; fourthly, Balancing of chances; fifthly, Victory."* The order listed here is Method, Measurement, Estimation, Calculation, Balancing and finally Victory. List the elements that are incorporated in your plan within each discipline:

   Measurement:

   Estimation:

   Calculation:

   Balancing of Chances:

   Victory:

14. *#18: "Measurement owes its existence to Earth; Estimation of quantity to Measurement; Calculation to Estimation of quantity; Balancing of chances to Calculation; and Victory to Balancing of chances."* Each of the elements you listed above is related. Expand upon how each within your specific plan is related.

15. *#19: "A victorious army opposed to a routed one, is as a pound's weight placed in the scale against a single grain."* *#20: "The onrush of a conquering force is like the burst-*

ing of pent-up waters into a chasm a thousand fathoms deep." These two tenets reference the power of intention in victory. Spend at least 5 minutes each day imagining how victory looks, smells, tastes, feels and sounds like, using all of your senses. Imagine it in the present tense, as if it is already happening, then allow yourself to feel gratitude for what is to come. Herein lies one of the greatest secrets to achieving victory in any endeavor in your life. Ideally journal about your experiences and that which you desire.

V.

Energy

1. Sun Tzu said: The control of a large force is the same principle as the control of a few men: it is merely a question of dividing up their numbers.

2. Fighting with a large army under your command is nowise different from fighting with a small one: it is merely a question of instituting signs and signals.

3. To ensure that your whole host may withstand the brunt of the enemy's attack and remain unshaken—this is affected by maneuvers direct and indirect.

4. That the impact of your army may be like a grindstone dashed against an egg—this is effected by the science of weak points and strong.

5. In all fighting, the direct method may be used for joining battle, but indirect methods will be needed in order to secure victory.

6. Indirect tactics, efficiently applied, are inexhaustible as Heaven and Earth, unending as the flow of rivers and streams; like the sun and moon, they end but to begin anew; like the four seasons, they pass away to return once more.

7. There are not more than five musical notes, yet the combinations of these five give rise to more melodies than can ever be heard.

8. There are not more than five primary colors (blue, yellow, red, white, and black), yet in combination they produce more hues than can ever been seen.

9. There are not more than five cardinal tastes (sour, acrid, salt, sweet, bitter), yet combinations of them yield more flavors than can ever be tasted.

10. In battle, there are not more than two methods of attack—the direct and the indirect; yet these two in combination give rise to an endless series of maneuvers.

11. The direct and the indirect lead on to each other in turn. It is like moving in a circle—you never come to an end. Who can exhaust the possibilities of their combination?

12. The onset of troops is like the rush of a torrent which will even roll stones along in its course.

13. The quality of decision is like the well-timed swoop of a falcon which enables it to strike and destroy its victim.

14. Therefore the good fighter will be terrible in his onset, and prompt in his decision.

15. Energy may be likened to the bending of a crossbow; decision, to the releasing of a trigger.

16. Amid the turmoil and tumult of battle, there may be seeming disorder and yet no real disorder at all; amid confusion and chaos, your array may be without head or tail, yet it will be proof against defeat.

17. Simulated disorder postulates perfect discipline, simulated fear postulates courage; simulated weakness postulates strength.

18. Hiding order beneath the cloak of disorder is simply a question of subdivision; concealing courage under a show of timidity presupposes a fund of latent energy; masking strength with weakness is to be effected by tactical dispositions.

19. Thus one who is skillful at keeping the enemy on the move maintains deceitful appearances, according to which the enemy will act. He sacrifices something, that the enemy may snatch at it.

20. By holding out baits, he keeps him on the march; then with a body of picked men he lies in wait for him.

21. The clever combatant looks to the effect of combined energy, and does not require too much from individuals. Hence his ability to pick out the right men and utilize combined energy.

22. When he utilizes combined energy, his fighting men become as it were like unto rolling logs or stones. For it is the nature of a log or stone to remain motionless on level ground, and to move when on a slope; if four-cornered, to come to a standstill, but if round-shaped, to go rolling down.

23. Thus the energy developed by good fighting men is as the momentum of a round stone rolled down a mountain thousands of feet in height. So much on the subject of energy.

V. Energy

In this chapter the master shares insights on how to use energy in your combat tactics. Stimulating all of your senses and using them to your strategic advantage is wise and builds strength in your tactical initiatives.

1. #1: *"Sun Tzu said: The control of a large force is the same principle as the control of a few men: it is merely a question of dividing up their numbers. #2: "Fighting with a large army under your command is nowise different from fighting with a small one: it is merely a question of instituting signs and signals."* Very often we quantify our desires, labeling them as being "too large to obtain" or "small, thus obtainable." Big or small, attainable or unobtainable is all a matter of your perception. If you believe your desires are too big to obtain, the world will reflect your belief. If you can't overcome your perception, then divide up your goals into smaller chunks that you believe are obtainable. Take one of your goals that you are currently struggling with and break it down into small steps. Write the steps out in as much detail as possible. Then take initiative, one step at a time.

2. #3: *"To ensure that your whole host may withstand the brunt of the enemy's attack and remain unshaken—this is affected by maneuvers direct and indirect."* How has your ego maneuvered itself indirectly in your life? Reflect on

how it disguised itself as being righteous and altruistic, when in fact its intent was to sabotage you. For example, while your heart wasn't really committed, you volunteered for a local cause because you thought it was the right thing to do. Your ego would say that your decision was thoughtful, kind and right. Upon reflection, however, if your decision was based on guilt and the sense that you "should" do so, then it was self-destructive as it was not heartfelt and did not energize you. In fact, following through on it most likely depleted your energy. Reflect and then write about a situation in which your ego indirectly maneuvered to defeat you.

3. *#4: "That the impact of your army may be like a grindstone dashed against an egg—this is effected by the science of weak points and strong."* Where are the weak points in your ego's initiatives? For example, do you have a wise friend who compassionately but honestly speaks out when your ego is thrusting its army upon your life? Write a list of your ego's weakest points.

4. *#5: "In all fighting, the direct method may be used for joining battle, but indirect methods will be needed in order to secure victory. #6: Indirect tactics, efficiently applied, are inexhaustible as Heaven and Earth, unending as the flow of rivers and streams; like the sun and moon, they end but to begin anew; like the four seasons, they pass away to return once more."* List the indirect methods you can use when fighting your ego. An example might be taking a walk in nature each day. While doing so does not directly combat your ego, it raises your spirit and your energy, which indirectly affects the way you fight it.

5. *#7: "There are not more than five musical notes, yet the combinations of these five give rise to more melodies*

than can ever be heard. #8: "There are not more than five primary colors (blue, yellow, red, white, and black), yet in combination they produce more hues than can ever been seen. #9: "There are not more than five cardinal tastes (sour, acrid, salt, sweet, bitter), yet combinations of them yield more flavors than can ever be tasted." Go through each of the three senses listed above, and correlate them to your life as you achieve victory over your ego. What color is victory? How does it taste? What does it sound like? Be as specific as possible, perhaps finding pictures, songs and foods that reflect the essence of it for you.

6. #10: "In battle, there are not more than two methods of attack—the direct and the indirect; yet these two in combination give rise to an endless series of maneuvers. #11: "The direct and the indirect lead on to each other in turn. It is like moving in a circle—you never come to an end. Who can exhaust the possibilities of their combination?" Each step you take in your life to find inner peace, whether direct or indirect, takes you one step closer to it. Keep a paper and pencil with you today, and list each maneuver, not matter how small or indirect it may seem. At the end of the day, review your list and note how each in combination is powerful and transformative.

7. #12: "The onset of troops is like the rush of a torrent which will even roll stones along in its course." Like rushing waters roll stones, each choice you make has a momentum and affects everything around you. Reflect again on the list you created in #5. Write how those choices affected others in your life. Did they then become a part of your army in your battle against your ego?

8. #13: "The quality of decision is like the well-timed swoop of a falcon which enables it to strike and destroy its vic-

tim. #14: *"Therefore the good fighter will be terrible in his onset, and prompt in his decision."* Promptness of decision does not allow for second-guessing yourself. Write a list of ways that you doubt or second-guess yourself. How does this get in the way of positive change in your life?

9. #15: *"Energy may be likened to the bending of a crossbow; decision, to the releasing of a trigger."* This tenet relates to making a decision and then letting go. If you continuously worry or again, second-guess your decision, it can lose momentum and is not energetically supported in a positive way. Do you struggle with letting go and relinquishing control? On a scale from one to ten (one being "very little" and ten being "very much so", rate how much do you struggle with letting go once you've made a decision?

1———2———3———4———5———6———7———8———9———10

10. #16: *"Amid the turmoil and tumult of battle, there may be seeming disorder and yet no real disorder at all; amid confusion and chaos, your array may be without head or tail, yet it will be proof against defeat."* Your ego often plays tricks on you, creating apparent confusion and disorder to create discontent within your mind. As Sun Tzu states there is "no real disorder". What do you currently do when you find yourself surrounded by chaos? What different steps can you take to ease your mind?

11. #17: *"Simulated disorder postulates perfect discipline, simulated fear postulates courage; simulated weakness postulates strength. #18: Hiding order beneath the cloak of disorder is simply a question of subdivision; concealing courage under a show of timidity presupposes a fund of latent energy; masking strength with weakness*

is to be effected by tactical dispositions." During times of apparent disorder, how do you practice discipline? When you are frightened, how do you find courage? When you believe yourself to be weak, how do you find strength?

12. *#19: "Thus one who is skillful at keeping the enemy on the move maintains deceitful appearances, according to which the enemy will act. He sacrifices something that the enemy may snatch at it. #20: "By holding out baits, he keeps him on the march; then with a body of picked men he lies in wait for him."* What have you sacrificed in order to gain victory in your battle against your ego? What are you willing to further sacrifice to do so?

13. *#21: "The clever combatant looks to the effect of combined energy, and does not require too much from individuals. Hence his ability to pick out the right men and utilize combined energy."* The principle makes reference to the power of *"combined energy"*. Often we can feel alone in our struggles, joining forces with other committed combatants can ease the burden and shed light on issues you may struggle with on your own. Write about your thoughts or experiences on the subject of sharing your burden with others.

14. *#22: "When he utilizes combined energy, his fighting men become as it were like unto rolling logs or stones. For it is the nature of a log or stone to remain motionless on level ground, and to move when on a slope; if four-cornered, to come to a standstill, but if round-shaped, to go rolling down. #23: "Thus the energy developed by good fighting men is as the momentum of a round stone rolled down a mountain thousands of feet in height. So much on the subject of energy."* Many personal growth systems emphasize that one or more unified when deal-

ing with an issue creates massive compounded strength and momentum. An example being AA or A Course in Miracles. Do some research on the power of combined forces in dealing with emotional challenges that you are combating. Write about your findings and if inspired, find an army of like-minded soldiers to join forces with.

VI.

Weak Points and Strong

1. Sun Tzu said: Whoever is first in the field and awaits the coming of the enemy, will be fresh for the fight; whoever is second in the field and has to hasten to battle will arrive exhausted.

2. Therefore the clever combatant imposes his will on the enemy, but does not allow the enemy's will to be imposed on him.

3. By holding out advantages to him, he can cause the enemy to approach of his own accord; or, by inflicting damage, he can make it impossible for the enemy to draw near.

4. If the enemy is taking his ease, he can harass him; if well supplied with food, he can starve him out; if quietly encamped, he can force him to move.

5. Appear at points which the enemy must hasten to defend; march swiftly to places where you are not expected.

6. An army may march great distances without distress, if it marches through country where the enemy is not.

7. You can be sure of succeeding in your attacks if you only attack places which are undefended. You can ensure the safety of your defense if you only hold positions that cannot be attacked.

8. Hence that general is skillful in attack whose opponent does not know what to defend; and he is skillful in defense whose opponent does not know what to attack.

9. O divine art of subtlety and secrecy! Through you we learn to be invisible, through you inaudible; and hence we can hold the enemy's fate in our hands.

10. You may advance and be absolutely irresistible, if you make for the enemy's weak points; you may retire and be safe from pursuit if your movements are more rapid than those of the enemy.

11. If we wish to fight, the enemy can be forced to an engagement even though he be sheltered behind a high rampart and a deep ditch. All we need do is

attack some other place that he will be obliged to relieve.

12. If we do not wish to fight, we can prevent the enemy from engaging us even though the lines of our encampment be merely traced out on the ground. All we need do is to throw something odd and unaccountable in his way.

13. By discovering the enemy's dispositions and remaining invisible ourselves, we can keep our forces concentrated, while the enemy's must be divided.

14. We can form a single united body, while the enemy must split up into fractions. Hence there will be a whole pitted against separate parts of a whole, which means that we shall be many to the enemy's few.

15. And if we are able thus to attack an inferior force with a superior one, our opponents will be in dire straits.

16. The spot where we intend to fight must not be made known; for then the enemy will have to prepare against a possible attack at several different points; and his forces being thus distributed in many directions, the numbers we shall have to face at any given point will be proportionately few.

17. For should the enemy strengthen his van, he will weaken his rear; should he strengthen his rear, he will weaken his van; should he strengthen his left, he will weaken his right; should he strengthen his right, he will weaken his left. If he sends reinforcements everywhere, he will everywhere be weak.

18. Numerical weakness comes from having to prepare against possible attacks; numerical strength, from compelling our adversary to make these preparations against us.

19. Knowing the place and the time of the coming battle, we may concentrate from the greatest distances in order to fight.

20. But if neither time nor place be known, then the left wing will be impotent to succor the right, the right equally impotent to succor the left, the van unable to relieve the rear, or the rear to support the van. How much more so if the furthest portions of the army are anything under a hundred LI apart, and even the nearest are separated by several LI!

21. Though according to my estimate the soldiers of Yueh exceed our own in number, that shall advantage them nothing in the matter of victory. I say then that victory can be achieved.

22. Though the enemy be stronger in numbers, we may prevent him from fighting. Scheme so as to discover his plans and the likelihood of their success.

23. Rouse him, and learn the principle of his activity or inactivity. Force him to reveal himself, so as to find out his vulnerable spots.

24. Carefully compare the opposing army with your own, so that you may know where strength is superabundant and where it is deficient.

25. In making tactical dispositions, the highest pitch you can attain is to conceal them; conceal your dispositions, and you will be safe from the prying of the subtlest spies, from the machinations of the wisest brains.

26. How victory may be produced for them out of the enemy's own tactics—that is what the multitude cannot comprehend.

27. All men can see the tactics whereby I conquer, but what none can see is the strategy out of which victory is evolved.

28. Do not repeat the tactics which have gained you one victory, but let your methods be regulated by the infinite variety of circumstances.

29. Military tactics are like unto water; for water in its natural course runs away from high places and hastens downwards.

30. So in war, the way is to avoid what is strong and to strike at what is weak.

31. Water shapes its course according to the nature of the ground over which it flows; the soldier works out his victory in relation to the foe whom he is facing.

32. Therefore, just as water retains no constant shape, so in warfare there are no constant conditions.

33. He who can modify his tactics in relation to his opponent and thereby succeed in winning, may be called a heaven-born captain.

34. The five elements (water, fire, wood, metal, earth) are not always equally predominant; the four seasons make way for each other in turn. There are short days and long; the moon has its periods of waning and waxing.

VI. *Weak Points and Strong*

How to focus your initiatives on your strengths and the weaknesses of your enemy is the central message of this chapter. By holding your ground and avoiding offensive tactics, you will have the upper hand in combat against your ego. For when you do not allow it to impose itself upon you, and you are aware of its antics, you allow it to weaken and expose itself to your stronger, higher self.

1. *#1: "Sun Tzu said: Whoever is first in the field and awaits the coming of the enemy, will be fresh for the fight; whoever is second in the field and has to hasten to battle will arrive exhausted."* Another tactic that our ego uses to create greater anxiety within us is creating situations where we are constantly rushing around, in a hurry. What is your relationship to time? Are you constantly late? Do you run from one task to another? On a scale from one to ten (one being "poor" and ten being "excellent", rate your current relationship with time.

1———2———3———4———5———6———7———8———9———10

2. *#2: "Therefore the clever combatant imposes his will on the enemy, but does not allow the enemy's will to be imposed on him."* What action steps can you take to make time your ally?

3. #3: *"By holding out advantages to him, he can cause the enemy to approach of his own accord; or, by inflicting damage, he can make it impossible for the enemy to draw near. #4: If the enemy is taking his ease, he can harass him; if well supplied with food, he can starve him out; if quietly encamped, he can force him to move."* How might you "starve out" you ego? For example, how might you totally disengage your inner critic?

4. #5: *"Appear at points which the enemy must hasten to defend; march swiftly to places where you are not expected."* Does your self-critic expect or anticipate kind non-judgment from you in response to its lashing out? Surprise it with responses of gentle understanding and kindness next time it lashes out at yourself or others. In the meantime write a letter of loving acceptance to your self-critic. Then meditate on your inner critic and ask it for a response.

5. #6: *"An army may march great distances without distress, if it marches through country where the enemy is not. #7: You can be sure of succeeding in your attacks if you only attack places which are undefended. You can ensure the safety of your defense if you only hold positions that cannot be attacked."* Surround yourself with people who are not your energy. Individuals raise your spirits and support you. When you hang around with critical and mean spirited people, you can get drawn into their negative energy. List three positive people you would enjoy spending more time with. Then make a point of including them more in your life.

6. #8: *"Hence that general is skillful in attack whose opponent does not know what to defend; and he is skillful in defense whose opponent does not know what to attack.#9: "O divine art of subtlety and secrecy! Through*

*you we learn to be invisible, through you inaudible; and
hence we can hold the enemy's fate in our hands."* How
do you remain invisible in your battle with your destructive self? The key to this tenet is "secrecy". As previously stated, when you spend time with negative people,
you can easily get drawn into their energy. Sharing the
musings of your critic with them fuels the fire at its core.
Often gossip and criticism flourish when negative people
gather. Take note next time you are in the company of
negative people, especially note when they speak criti-
cally of others. Make a conscious choice not to engage
in the negative conversation. Write about your findings in
doing so.

7. #10: *"You may advance and be absolutely irresistible, if
you make for the enemy's weak points; you may retire
and be safe from pursuit if your movements are more
rapid than those of the enemy. #11: If we wish to fight,
the enemy can be forced to an engagement even though
he be sheltered behind a high rampart and a deep ditch.
All we need do is attack some other place that he will
be obliged to relieve. #12: If we do not wish to fight, we
can prevent the enemy from engaging us even though
the lines of our encampment be merely traced out on the
ground. All we need do is to throw something odd and
unaccountable in his way."* You might experiment with
"rapid movements" when surrounded by negative gossip. Play with shifting the conversation to more positive
topics. Watch and note if the energy gets pulled back into
negativity again. Write about your findings, especially
noting how patterns arise.

8. #13: *"By discovering the enemy's dispositions and remaining invisible ourselves, we can keep our forces concentrated, while the enemy's must be divided. #14: We can*

form a single united body, while the enemy must split up into fractions. Hence there will be a whole pitted against separate parts of a whole, which means that we shall be many to the enemy's few. #15: And if we are able thus to attack an inferior force with a superior one, our opponents will be in dire straits." Do not under-estimate the might of your intentions. Putting your attention on your intention is a very powerful strategy in winning at whatever battle you find yourself involved. Keeping your focus on your intention creates the "whole" that divides and weakens the enemy force, your ego. If you are not already doing so, write out your intention in three sentences or less, and then speak it aloud each day in the morning when you arise and before you go to bed. Say it with conviction and power.

9. *#16: "The spot where we intend to fight must not be made known; for then the enemy will have to prepare against a possible attack at several different points; and his forces being thus distributed in many directions, the numbers we shall have to face at any given point will be proportionately few. #17: For should the enemy strengthen his van, he will weaken his rear; should he strengthen his rear, he will weaken his van; should he strengthen his left, he will weaken his right; should he strengthen his right, he will weaken his left. If he sends reinforcements everywhere, he will everywhere be weak."* Sometimes you weaken yourself when you share your inner battle with others who are not supportive and similarly committed. Keep your battle plan to yourself and find the confidence within yourself to know that it is working.

10. *#18: "Numerical weakness comes from having to prepare against possible attacks; numerical strength, from compelling our adversary to make these preparations against*

us. #19: Knowing the place and the time of the coming battle, we may concentrate from the greatest distances in order to fight." You know your ego and how it works. You have seen it in action for many years and can anticipate the "place and time" that it will fight you. Whenever possible, anticipate potential situations before they arise, and prior, talk to your insecurities, ensuring them that victory is imminent. For example, if you know you struggle with a family member and they are coming to dinner, make a commitment to be nonreactive. Imagine yourself calm and unresponsive to any negativity they bring your way. Write about your experience after practicing this strategy.

11. *#20: "But if neither time nor place be known, then the left wing will be impotent to succor the right, the right equally impotent to succor the left, the van unable to relieve the rear, or the rear to support the van. How much more so if the furthest portions of the army are anything under a hundred LI apart, and even the nearest are separated by several LI!"* If you practice non-reactivity when your ego is being challenged, the enemy will become impotent. Write a list of the things that you react to; people or situations that trigger your anger, frustration or anxiety.

12. *#21: "Though according to my estimate the soldiers of Yueh exceed our own in number, that shall advantage them nothing in the matter of victory. I say then that victory can be achieved."* Now that you have your list and are clear, the ego is weaker. As you note new triggers, add them to the list, and have confidence that knowing the triggers or strategies of the ego empowers you.

13. *#22: "Though the enemy be stronger in numbers, we may prevent him from fighting. Scheme so as to discover his plans and the likelihood of their success. #23: "Rouse*

him, and learn the principle of his activity or inactivity. Force him to reveal himself, so as to find out his vulnerable spots." In response to each trigger on the list you created in #11, write clam and non-reactive ways that you can respond to each.

14. #24: *"Carefully compare the opposing army with your own, so that you may know where strength is superabundant and where it is deficient. #25: In making tactical dispositions, the highest pitch you can attain is to conceal them; conceal your dispositions, and you will be safe from the prying of the subtlest spies, from the machinations of the wisest brains."* Sometimes you have to fake it until you make it. There is often a dance between yourself and those who trigger reactions from you. One of your best weapons is non-response. If you are no longer triggered or reactive to their annoyances, they are disempowered. The next time you meet with someone who you find difficult to deal with, "act" as if they do not bother you. "Act" as if you enjoy their company. If they say negative or critical things, laugh and "act" like you are enjoying the repartee. Write about your experience.

15. #26 *"How victory may be produced for them out of the enemy's own tactics—that is what the multitude cannot comprehend."* As previously mentioned, often what annoys us in others is a habit or character traits that we have disowned in ourselves. Another tactic is to focus on what we appreciate about the individual. Write the name of someone who annoys you. Then write a list of all of the traits that you respect and appreciate about them. Each day, until you see them again, focus on the list of positive traits and attributes that they possess. Note any changes about your feelings towards them after doing this exercise.

16. #27: *"All men can see the tactics whereby I conquer, but what none can see is the strategy out of which victory is evolved."* While others may see a shift in your disposition, they may not know why. If anyone notes the shift, or say something positive and affirming, write it down. It is important that you keep a journal of your victories, and read it often (especially when you are feeling defeated or exhausted).

17. #28: *"Do not repeat the tactics which have gained you one victory, but let your methods be regulated by the infinite variety of circumstances."* What other methods can you use to respond to people or situations that trigger your ego? For example, waiting in traffic. Does this make you impatient and angry? How might you tactically defeat the frustration? You might play educational audio programs in your car, so that when you are stuck in traffic, you feel more empowered and proactive. List any tactics you can come up with, and give them a try.

18. #29: *"Military tactics are like unto water; for water in its natural course runs away from high places and hastens downwards. #30: So in war, the way is to avoid what is strong and to strike at what is weak."* Some people will trigger you, no matter how hard you try not to react to their negativity. Your best tactic is to avoid them whenever possible. Do an inventory of the people in your life. Write a list of those with whom you feel drained when you are in their presence.

19. #31: *"Water shapes its course according to the nature of the ground over which it flows; the soldier works out his victory in relation to the foe whom he is facing."* Go through the list you created in #29. Sometimes we grow out of friendships. Are there "foe" that you no longer

choose to face? Are there individuals in your life who no longer energetically match with you? List them below.

20. *#32: "Therefore, just as water retains no constant shape, so in warfare there are no constant conditions. #33: He who can modify his tactics in relation to his opponent and thereby succeed in winning, may be called a heaven-born captain."* For a period of time, you may wish to stay away from those with whom you find yourself drained when in their presence. Someday you may find you can "modify your tactics". As you gain strength over your ego, you may be able to bring them back into your life. However, you may not want to. Know this, and have the confidence to care for yourself in the best way possible.

21. *#34: "The five elements (water, fire, wood, metal, earth) are not always equally predominant; the four seasons make way for each other in turn. There are short days and long; the moon has its periods of waning and waxing."* Life changes, and we change. Know that those who trigger you are also on their own emotional journey—fighting their own internal battles. Allow for the changes in them, like the changing of the seasons. Give yourself and others permission to grow. Write about any changes that you note in yourself since you began this process.

VII.

Maneuvering

1. Sun Tzu said: In war, the general receives his commands from the sovereign.

2. Having collected an army and concentrated his forces, he must blend and harmonize the different elements thereof before pitching his camp.

3. After that, comes tactical maneuvering, than which there is nothing more difficult. The difficulty of tactical maneuvering consists in turning the devious into the direct, and misfortune into gain.

4. Thus, to take a long and circuitous route, after enticing the enemy out of the way, and though starting after him, to contrive to reach the goal before him, shows knowledge of the artifice of *deviation*.

5. Maneuvering with an army is advantageous; with an undisciplined multitude, most dangerous.

6. If you set a fully equipped army in march in order to snatch an advantage, the chances are that you will be too late. On the other hand, to detach a flying column for the purpose involves the sacrifice of its baggage and stores.

7. Thus, if you order your men to roll up their buff-coats, and make forced marches without halting day or night, covering double the usual distance at a stretch, doing a hundred LI in order to wrest an advantage, the leaders of all your three divisions will fall into the hands of the enemy.

8. The stronger men will be in front, the jaded ones will fall behind, and on this plan only one-tenth of your army will reach its destination.

9. If you march fifty LI in order to outmaneuver the enemy, you will lose the leader of your first division, and only half your force will reach the goal.

10. If you march thirty LI with the same object, two-thirds of your army will arrive.

11. We may take it then that an army without its baggage-train is lost; without provisions it is lost; without bases of supply it is lost.

12. We cannot enter into alliances until we are acquainted with the designs of our neighbors.

13. We are not fit to lead an army on the march unless we are familiar with the face of the country—its mountains and forests, its pitfalls and precipices, its marshes and swamps.

14. We shall be unable to turn natural advantage to account unless we make use of local guides.

15. In war, practice dissimulation, and you will succeed.

16. Whether to concentrate or to divide your troops, must be decided by circumstances.

17. Let your rapidity be that of the wind, your compactness that of the forest.

18. In raiding and plundering be like fire, is immovability like a mountain.

19. Let your plans be dark and impenetrable as night, and when you move, fall like a thunderbolt.

20. When you plunder a countryside, let the spoil be divided amongst your men; when you capture new territory, cut it up into allotments for the benefit of the soldiery.

21. Ponder and deliberate before you make a move.

22. He will conquer who has learnt the artifice of devi-
     ation. Such is the art of maneuvering.

23. The Book of Army Management says: On the field
     of battle, the spoken word does not carry far enough:
     hence the institution of gongs and drums. Nor can
     ordinary objects be seen clearly enough: hence the
     institution of banners and flags.

24. Gongs and drums, banners and flags, are means
     whereby the ears and eyes of the host may be fo-
     cused on one particular point.

25. The host thus forming a single united body, is it im-
     possible either for the brave to advance alone, or for
     the cowardly to retreat alone. This is the art of han-
     dling large masses of men.

26. In night-fighting, then, make much use of sig-
     nal-fires and drums, and in fighting by day, of flags
     and banners, as a means of influencing the ears and
     eyes of your army.

27. A whole army may be robbed of its spirit; a com-
     mander-in-chief may be robbed of his presence of
     mind.

28. Now a soldier's spirit is keenest in the morning; by noonday it has begun to flag; and in the evening, his mind is bent only on returning to camp.

29. A clever general, therefore, avoids an army when its spirit is keen, but attacks it when it is sluggish and inclined to return. This is the art of studying moods.

30. Disciplined and calm, to await the appearance of disorder and hubbub amongst the enemy: this is the art of retaining self-possession.

31. To be near the goal while the enemy is still far from it, to wait at ease while the enemy is toiling and struggling, to be well-fed while the enemy is famished: this is the art of husbanding one's strength.

32. To refrain from intercepting an enemy whose banners are in perfect order, to refrain from attacking an army drawn up in calm and confident array: this is the art of studying circumstances.

33. It is a military axiom not to advance uphill against the enemy, nor to oppose him when he comes downhill.

34. Do not pursue an enemy who simulates flight; do not attack soldiers whose temper is keen.

35. Do not swallow bait offered by the enemy. Do not
     interfere with an army that is returning home.

36. When you surround an army, leave an outlet free.
     Do not press a desperate foe too hard.

37. Such is the art of warfare.

VII. Maneuvering

In this chapter, Sun Tzu discusses the art of tactical maneuvering. When you are aware of your surroundings, you allow the elements to work on your behalf. Such is true with your ego. If you have insights about the enemy and are aware of those things that trigger you, you are better able to win your battle with your reactive and fearful ego.

1. *#1: "Sun Tzu said: In war, the general receives his commands from the sovereign."* Where do you believe you are receiving the commands you are following in this battle with your ego? Are you being given guidance by your wise inner self, a higher power, or by some other form?

2. *#2: "Having collected an army and concentrated his forces, he must blend and harmonize the different elements thereof before pitching his camp."* Before getting started on your journey towards inner peace, you must be in total alignment with healing yourself. You must create the time, space and intention to win over your ego. Do a check-in. Is there any part of you that is not totally committed to finding greater peace? Write about your discoveries as you do this reflection.

3. *#3: "After that, comes tactical maneuvering, than which there is nothing more difficult. The difficulty of tactical maneuvering consists in turning the devious into the*

direct, and misfortune into gain." How can you turn misfortunes in your life into "gains"? Reflect on challenges you have faced in the past. In retrospect, how do you now see them as helpful in your life? Did you experience personal growth in response to them? Did you learn something new about yourself, or develop a new skill? Write about an experience where you felt you "gained" from experiencing it.

4. #4: *"Thus, to take a long and circuitous route, after enticing the enemy out of the way, and though starting after him, to contrive to reach the goal before him, shows knowledge of the artifice of deviation."* Sometime the "long and circuitous" route to healing our ego issues is the wisest. Expecting immediate results is very often a trick of the ego—a means to further beating yourself up. Are you hard on yourself when you make a mistake or do not achieve immediate results? Write about the ways in which you are hard on yourself.

5. #5: *"Maneuvering with an army is advantageous; with an undisciplined multitude, most dangerous. #6: If you set a fully equipped army in march in order to snatch an advantage, the chances are that you will be too late. On the other hand, to detach a flying column for the purpose involves the sacrifice of its baggage and stores."* While it takes discipline to battle your ego, you need to take immediate action. Waiting until everything is "perfect" is another ego trap. Is there any practice or activity you are currently eager to pursue, but have decided that "I'm not ready yet. First I need to be completely prepared and have all of my ducks in a row." Write a list of items that you are enthusiastic to pursue, but are holding off on starting because you don't feel ready.

6. #7: *"Thus, if you order your men to roll up their buff-coats, and make forced marches without halting day or night, covering double the usual distance at a stretch, doing a hundred LI in order to wrest an advantage, the leaders of all your three divisions will fall into the hands of the enemy. #8: "The stronger men will be in front, the jaded ones will fall behind, and on this plan only one-tenth of your army will reach its destination."* If you exhaust yourself in your endeavors, you will also fail. Finding balance in your life is key to achieving success. Do you have enough "down" time? Do you get enough quality sleep each night? Do you have ample recreation time in your day? Do you eat right? Write a list of the ways in which you do not have balance in your life.

7. #9: *"If you march fifty LI in order to outmaneuver the enemy, you will lose the leader of your first division, and only half your force will reach the goal. #10: "If you march thirty LI with the same object, two-thirds of your army will arrive."* Write at least three action steps you can take to achieve greater balance and "down time" in your life. Then commit to taking these steps. Keep a journal each day, listing the steps you have taken towards balancing your life.

8. #11: *"We may take it then that an army without its baggage-train is lost; without provisions it is lost; without bases of supply it is lost."* If you take the "provisions" away from your ego, it has no sustenance. Write a list of the things that "feed" your ego. For example, joining in competition, gossip, stress, fatigue or lack of sleep, etc.

9. #12: *"We cannot enter into alliances until we are acquainted with the designs of our neighbors."* You must be able to see the ego at work in those around you, as well as in yourself. For the next day, keep a journal of situations where

you see your co-worker's, family member's and friend's egos at play.

10. *#13: "We are not fit to lead an army on the march unless we are familiar with the face of the country—its mountains and forests, its pitfalls and precipices, its marshes and swamps."* You need to know the terrain of your battlefield and its surroundings. Where does your ego flourish most at work, at home, and in social situations? Write a list of the triggers that power your ego in these three terrains.

11. *#14: "We shall be unable to turn natural advantage to account unless we make use of local guides."* It is important that you make use of the "local guides", those who are knowledgeable about the terrain you are about to inhabit. It is true that knowledge is power. Take some time to read books or listen to audio programs about psychology and inner conflict. Write about at least one research document that you have investigated.

12. *#15: "In war, practice dissimulation, and you will succeed. #16: Whether to concentrate or to divide your troops, must be decided by circumstances."* Whether you focus your energy on one particular aspect of your ego, or divide your focus, and work on all of them, is up to you. Whatever your strategy, commit to it completely. Do you plan on battling one aspect of your ego (judgment, control, anger, resentment, etc.), or one in particular? Describe your plan of attack.

13. *#17: "Let your rapidity be that of the wind, your compactness that of the forest. #18: In raiding and plundering be like fire, is immovability like a mountain. #19: Let your plans be dark and impenetrable as night, and when you move, fall like a thunderbolt."* Your ego is very cunning. You will find that it can mask itself as righteous and altruistic,

while, in fact, it is being cruel and critical. Be ready for it, and watch for the trickery. Write a list of ways that it tricks you. As you pay attention to this, keep adding to the list.

14. #20: *"When you plunder a countryside, let the spoil be divided amongst your men; when you capture new territory, cut it up into allotments for the benefit of the soldiery. #21: Ponder and deliberate before you make a move. #22: He will conquer who has learnt the artifice of deviation. Such is the art of maneuvering."* It is important that you feed your self-esteem. As you find yourself confronting your ego, be sure to acknowledge your achievements. Write a list of the ways that you noted you successfully took steps towards confronting your ego this week. Ideally, keep a journal that focuses on all of the improvements you are making in your life.

15. #23: *"The Book of Army Management says: On the field of battle, the spoken word does not carry far enough: hence the institution of gongs and drums. Nor can ordinary objects be seen clearly enough: hence the institution of banners and flags. #24:"Gongs and drums, banners and flags, are means whereby the ears and eyes of the host may be focused on one particular point. #25: The host thus forming a single united body, is it impossible either for the brave to advance alone, or for the cowardly to retreat alone. This is the art of handling large masses of men. #26: In night-fighting, then, make much use of signal-fires and drums, and in fighting by day, of flags and banners, as a means of influencing the ears and eyes of your army."* Gong, drums, banners and flags are all tools with which the forces can remain focused and united in their approach. What tools do you have in your plan that will assist you in remaining focused? An example is a journal. That which you focus on and write about magni-

fies. If you keep a journal listing your strategies, your victories, your fellow commanders (supportive individuals) and the enemy line (triggers, unresolved issues that you are still working on), you will gain strength and clarity. If you haven't already done so, journal daily before going to sleep, focusing particularly on your day's successes.

16. *#27: "A whole army may be robbed of its spirit; a commander-in-chief may be robbed of his presence of mind. #28:Now a soldier's spirit is keenest in the morning; by noonday it has begun to flag; and in the evening, his mind is bent only on returning to camp. #29:A clever general, therefore, avoids an army when its spirit is keen, but attacks it when it is sluggish and inclined to return. This is the art of studying moods."* In the morning, when your army is "keenest", before you get out of bed, take some deep breaths and focus on your intentions for the day. Imagine a day that is peaceful, easy and trigger-free. If you have the time, write out your intention for the day.

17. *#30: "Disciplined and calm, to await the appearance of disorder and hubbub amongst the enemy: this is the art of retaining self-possession. #31: To be near the goal while the enemy is still far from it, to wait at ease while the enemy is toiling and struggling, to be well-fed while the enemy is famished: this is the art of husbanding one's strength."* How might you further cultivate non-reactivity and self-possession when you find yourself triggered? One idea is to wear a rubber band on your wrist. Whenever you note yourself being triggered, before taking action, pull on the band as a reminder that you need not react. Sometimes practicing a simple technique like this can provide you with a couple of seconds to pull your focus away from what is making you react. Try this technique or another and write about your experience.

18. *#32: "To refrain from intercepting an enemy whose banners are in perfect order, to refrain from attacking an army drawn up in calm and confident array: this is the art of studying circumstances. #33: "It is a military axiom not to advance uphill against the enemy, nor to oppose him when he comes downhill. #34: Do not pursue an enemy who simulates flight; do not attack soldiers whose temper is keen."* These are all sound strategies that suggest that you avoid attacking an army that is in full strength. Sometimes your ego may react, display itself in full strength. That may not be the time to respond, as often it is difficult to do so at that time. Again, this is where reflection is beneficial. Find a time each day (ideally the same time each day), and do some deep breathing. Fill yourself with words of encouragement, compassion and respect. Speak to yourself as you would a struggling child—with compassion and pride. Try doing this exercise each day for at least a month. Write about its affects on your sense of self.

19. *#35: "Do not swallow bait offered by the enemy. Do not interfere with an army that is returning home. #36: When you surround an army, leave an outlet free. Do not press a desperate foe too hard. #37: Such is the art of warfare."* You need to know when to retreat when battling your ego. If you find yourself lashing out in reaction to a situation and are not able to retreat at that time, give yourself a break, knowing that you did your best. Focusing 24-7 without giving yourself a break can create an obsessive drive. Find balance and rest, knowing that you are doing the best that you can at this time. Write about at least three things you do that provide you with rest and a focal point that does not revolve around your self-improvement directives. Then try to do them at least once each week.

VIII.

Variation In Tactics

1. Sun Tzu said: In war, the general receives his commands from the sovereign, collects his army and concentrates his forces

2. When in difficult country, do not encamp. In country where high roads intersect, join hands with your allies. Do not linger in dangerously isolated positions. In hemmed-in situations, you must resort to stratagem. In desperate position, you must fight.

3. There are roads which must not be followed, armies which must be not attacked, towns which must be besieged, positions which must not be contested, commands of the sovereign which must not be obeyed.

4. The general who thoroughly understands the advantages that accompany variation of tactics knows how to handle his troops.

5. The general who does not understand these, may be well acquainted with the configuration of the country, yet he will not be able to turn his knowledge to practical account.

6. So, the student of war who is unversed in the art of war of varying his plans, even though he be acquainted with the Five Advantages, will fail to make the best use of his men.

7. Hence in the wise leader's plans, considerations of advantage and of disadvantage will be blended together.

8. If our expectation of advantage be tempered in this way, we may succeed in accomplishing the essential part of our schemes.

9. If, on the other hand, in the midst of difficulties we are always ready to seize an advantage, we may extricate ourselves from misfortune.

10. Reduce the hostile chiefs by inflicting damage on them; and make trouble for them, and keep them constantly engaged; hold out specious allurements, and make them rush to any given point.

11. The art of war teaches us to rely not on the likelihood of the enemy's not coming, but on our own

readiness to receive him; not on the chance of his not attacking, but rather on the fact that we have made our position unassailable.

12. There are five dangerous faults which may affect a general:
    (1) Recklessness, which leads to destruction;
    (2) cowardice, which leads to capture;
    (3) a hasty temper, which can be provoked by insults;
    (4) a delicacy of honor which is sensitive to shame;
    (5) over-solicitude for his men, which exposes him to worry and trouble.

13. These are the five besetting sins of a general, ruinous to the conduct of war.

14. When an army is overthrown and its leader slain, the cause will surely be found among these five dangerous faults. Let them be a subject of meditation.

VIII. *Variations In Tactics*

Being fluid in your initiatives and being open to variations in your tactics, you are in a stronger position to fight and win over your ego. Restriction and rigidity do not allow for the unexpected and a cunning enemy would attempt to throw you with unexpected maneuvers. In this chapter, Sun Tzu provides detailed strategies that evolve around fluidity and variation. He also sheds insights on the five dangerous faults that can weaken a general's position.

1. #1: *"Sun Tzu said: In war, the general receives his commands from the sovereign, collects his army and concentrates his forces. #2: When in difficult country, do not encamp. In country where high roads intersect, join hands with your allies. Do not linger in dangerously isolated positions. In hemmed-in situations, you must resort to stratagem. In desperate position, you must fight."* When the ego, especially the self-critic is feeling trapped, it often isolates itself. You emotionally beat yourself up, and tell yourself that you are not good company for others. Do you have a tendency to isolate yourself when you are struggling most with your ego? If so, how?

2. #3: *"There are roads which must not be followed, armies which must be not attacked, towns which must be besieged, positions which must not be contested, com-*

mands of the sovereign which must not be obeyed." You are the commander of your own journey. Very often our ego creates a distrust of ourselves. We give others power over us, thinking that they know better. As you win over your ego, you will start to feel more empowered and you will trust your own inner knowing more. Make a commitment here and now to start listening more to your inner knowing. When others give you suggestions, thank them, but do not take their message to heart unless it rings true for you. For the next week, take advice from no one and focus on trusting your knowing. Write about your experience.

3. *#4: "The general who thoroughly understands the advantages that accompany variation of tactics knows how to handle his troops. #5: The general who does not understand these, may be well acquainted with the configuration of the country, yet he will not be able to turn his knowledge to practical account."* Your ego is cunning, so ideally you want a "variation of tactics" in your battle plans. Research on new tactics you could engage upon at this point in your plan. There are many techniques and modalities in the self-help movement. Spend at least 15 minutes and explore alternative means of dealing with your ego challenges. Write about your findings.

4. *#6: "So, the student of war who is unversed in the art of war of varying his plans, even though he be acquainted with the Five Advantages, will fail to make the best use of his men. #7: "Hence in the wise leader's plans, considerations of advantage and of disadvantage will be blended together."* Do an inventory of the techniques you are currently practicing to fight your ego. Then mark those that you have noted are working, and those that are not. If a

technique is not working, reflect on why, and if you don't believe it will be successful, do not practice it any longer. Be sure, however, to replace it with an alternative technique. Experiment and see what works best for you.

5. #8: *"If our expectation of advantage be tempered in this way, we may succeed in accomplishing the essential part of our schemes."* Expectation is key to your success in any endeavor you pursue. If you expect and can imagine yourself succeeding, and if you take the necessary steps to follow through on your plans, you will likely succeed. Take a deep look into your expectations around beating your ego. Do you truly believe you can? If so, when? If not, what is blocking you. Do an inventory on your expectations and write about your findings.

6. #9: *"If, on the other hand, in the midst of difficulties we are always ready to seize an advantage, we may extricate ourselves from misfortune."* When you are in the midst of challenges, look for the "advantages" that may arise at that time. Often while things appear to be working against us, they are not. For example, we often hear stories about people who are devastated when they lose their job, only to find that they end up getting an even better job out of the situation. Reflect on your life, and come up with at least two situations that you thought were negative, however turned out in your favor.

7. #10: *"Reduce the hostile chiefs by inflicting damage on them; and make trouble for them, and keep them constantly engaged; hold out specious allurements, and make them rush to any given point."* How might you further tempt your ego to become more compliant? What "allurements" can you offer that would keep it engaged?

8. *#11: "The art of war teaches us to rely not on the likelihood of the enemy's not coming, but on our own readiness to receive him; not on the chance of his not attacking, but rather on the fact that we have made our position unassailable."* If you commit to total compassion and understanding towards yourself and others, whatever your ego's position, the anger and torment melts away, you position becomes unassailable. Of course, finding compassion in the heat of emotional triggers can be difficult. At times you will have to fake it until you make it. Try doing so the next time you are judging yourself and/or another. Let the judgment melt away as you imagine yourself and others you are struggling with as children in a schoolyard, all trying desperately to be seen and understood. Write about your experience.

9. *#12: "There are five dangerous faults which may affect a general: (1) Recklessness, which leads to destruction; 2) cowardice, which leads to capture; (3) a hasty temper, which can be provoked by insults; (4) a delicacy of honor which is sensitive to shame; (5) over-solicitude for his men, which exposes him to worry and trouble. #13: "These are the five besetting sins of a general, ruinous to the conduct of war."* Review the "five dangerous faults" and reflect on how you fall into them in your daily life. 1) When are you reckless and inattentive and how does the recklessness sabotage you? 2) When are you cowardly, and how do you feel about yourself after behaving as such? 3) When do you lose your temper? What provokes you to do so? 4) When do you find your pride and subsequent shame in full play? 5) When do you spend too much time worrying about your parents, children, spouse or friends? Is worry helpful? Is it another distraction that takes you away from living the life that you want?

10. *#14: "When an army is overthrown and its leader slain, the cause will surely be found among these five dangerous faults. Let them be a subject of meditation."* Take time to meditate on each of the five reflective questions in #13. See how they sabotage you, and then see yourself shifting away from them. Write about what you experience in your meditation.

IX.

The Army On the March

1. Sun Tzu said: We come now to the question of encamping the army, and observing signs of the enemy. Pass quickly over mountains, and keep in the neighborhood of valleys.

2. Camp in high places, facing the sun. Do not climb heights in order to fight. So much for mountain warfare.

3. After crossing a river, you should get far away from it.

4. When an invading force crosses a river in its onward march, do not advance to meet it in mid-stream. It will be best to let half the army get across, and then deliver your attack.

5. If you are anxious to fight, you should not go to meet the invader near a river which he has to cross.

6. Moor your craft higher up than the enemy, and facing the sun. Do not move up-stream to meet the enemy. So much for river warfare.

7. In crossing salt-marshes, your sole concern should be to get over them quickly, without any delay.

8. If forced to fight in a salt-marsh, you should have water and grass near you, and get your back to a clump of trees. So much for operations in salt-marches.

9. In dry, level country, take up an easily accessible position with rising ground to your right and on your rear, so that the danger may be in front, and safety lie behind. So much for campaigning in flat country.

10. These are the four useful branches of military knowledge which enabled the Yellow Emperor to vanquish four several sovereigns.

11. All armies prefer high ground to low and sunny places to dark.

12. If you are careful of your men, and camp on hard ground, the army will be free from disease of every kind, and this will spell victory.

13. When you come to a hill or a bank, occupy the sunny side, with the slope on your right rear. Thus

you will at once act for the benefit of your soldiers and utilize the natural advantages of the ground.

14. When, in consequence of heavy rains up-country, a river which you wish to ford is swollen and flecked with foam, you must wait until it subsides.

15. Country in which there are precipitous cliffs with torrents running between, deep natural hollows, confined places, tangled thickets, quagmires and crevasses, should be left with all possible speed and not approached.

16. While we keep away from such places, we should get the enemy to approach them; while we face them, we should let the enemy have them on his rear.

17. If in the neighborhood of your camp there should be any hilly country, ponds surrounded by aquatic grass, hollow basins filled with reeds, or woods with thick undergrowth, they must be carefully routed out and searched; for these are places where men in ambush or insidious spies are likely to be lurking.

18. When the enemy is close at hand and remains quiet, he is relying on the natural strength of his position.

19. When he keeps aloof and tries to provoke a battle, he is anxious for the other side to advance.

20. If his place of encampment is easy of access, he is tendering a bait.

21. Movement amongst the trees of a forest shows that the enemy is advancing. The appearance of a number of screens in the midst of thick grass means that the enemy wants to make us suspicious.

22. The rising of birds in their flight is the sign of an ambuscade. Startled beasts indicate that a sudden attack is coming.

23. When there is dust rising in a high column, it is the sign of chariots advancing; when the dust is low, but spread over a wide area, it betokens the approach of infantry. When it branches out in different directions, it shows that parties have been sent to collect firewood. A few clouds of dust moving to and fro signify that the army is encamping.

24. Humble words and increased preparations are signs that the enemy is about to advance. Violent language and driving forward as if to the attack are signs that he will retreat.

25. When the light chariots come out first and take up a position on the wings, it is a sign that the enemy is forming for battle.

26. Peace proposals unaccompanied by a sworn covenant indicate a plot.

27. When there is much running about and the soldiers fall into rank, it means that the critical moment has come.

28. When some are seen advancing and some retreating, it is a lure.

29. When the soldiers stand leaning on their spears, they are faint from want of food.

30. If those who are sent to draw water begin by drinking themselves, the army is suffering from thirst.

31. If the enemy sees an advantage to be gained and makes no effort to secure it, the soldiers are exhausted.

32. If birds gather on any spot, it is unoccupied. Clamor by night betokens nervousness.

33. If there is disturbance in the camp, the general's authority is weak. If the banners and flags are shifted about, sedition is afoot. If the officers are angry, it means that the men are weary.

34. When an army feeds its horses with grain and kills its cattle for food, and when the men do not hang their cooking-pots over the camp-fires, showing that they will not return to their tents, you may know that they are determined to fight to the death.

35. The sight of men whispering together in small knots or speaking in subdued tones points to disaffection amongst the rank and file.

36. Too frequent rewards signify that the enemy is at the end of his resources; too many punishments betray a condition of dire distress.

37. To begin by bluster, but afterwards to take fright at the enemy's numbers, shows a supreme lack of intelligence.

38. When envoys are sent with compliments in their mouths, it is a sign that the enemy wishes for a truce.

39. If the enemy's troops march up angrily and remain facing ours for a long time without either joining battle or taking themselves off again, the situation is one that demands great vigilance and circumspection.

40. If our troops are no more in number than the enemy, that is amply sufficient; it only means that no direct attack can be made. What we can do is simply to concentrate all our available strength, keep a close watch on the enemy, and obtain reinforcements.

41. He who exercises no forethought but makes light of his opponents is sure to be captured by them.

42. If soldiers are punished before they have grown attached to you, they will not prove submissive; and, unless submissive, then will be practically useless. If, when the soldiers have become attached to you, punishments are not enforced, they will still be unless.

43. Therefore soldiers must be treated in the first instance with humanity, but kept under control by means of iron discipline. This is a certain road to victory.

44. If in training soldiers commands are habitually enforced, the army will be well-disciplined; if not, its discipline will be bad.

45. If a general shows confidence in his men but always insists on his orders being obeyed, the gain will be mutual.

STUDY GUIDE

IX. The Army On the March

This is the point of action in you battle initiatives. In this chapter Sun Tzu shares strategies that you would be wise to follow once your army is marching and on the move. When you take action against your ego, you must know the terrain upon which you will be doing battle. Having an awareness of what the playing field is, and how you can anticipate the strategies of your ego, the better your chances of victory will be.

1. *#1: "Sun Tzu said: We come now to the question of encamping the army, and observing signs of the enemy. Pass quickly over mountains, and keep in the neighborhood of valleys. #2: Camp in high places, facing the sun. Do not climb heights in order to fight. So much for mountain warfare."* This strategy suggests that you lay low and remain visible to the enemy as little as possible. Relating this to the battle with your ego, how do you "keep in the neighborhood of the valleys"? At times it is important that you keep your emotional work private. If it is shared with the wrong people, unfortunately, those who are struggling with their own ego can use the knowledge of your issues to trigger you. Make a list of anyone with whom you have shared your emotional challenges with, that you shouldn't have. Then make an effort to stop doing so in the future.

2. #3: *"After crossing a river, you should get far away from it. #4: When an invading force crosses a river in its onward march, do not advance to meet it in mid-stream. It will be best to let half the army get across, and then deliver your attack. #5: If you are anxious to fight, you should not go to meet the invader near a river which he has to cross. #6: Moor your craft higher up than the enemy, and facing the sun. Do not move up-stream to meet the enemy. So much for river warfare."* In this case the analogy of the river is another place of vulnerability. If you consider it, water slows you down if you are being pursued. If you are the pursuant, then it could work in your favor. Are there times when you think you would be better to slow down on your attack of the ego? At times, especially if you tend to be a perfectionist, you may over-work yourself to the point of exhaustion. Try one week of slowing down. Do not read or watch any self-help material, and allow yourself to be fully present and experience things as they arise. See if you can let go of your self-analysis and just be. At the end of the week, write about your findings.

3. #7: *"In crossing salt-marshes, your sole concern should be to get over them quickly, without any delay. #8: "If forced to fight in a salt-marsh, you should have water and grass near you, and get your back to a clump of trees. So much for operations in salt-marches."* When you think of salt-marshes, you have salt-water that slows you down, along with high standing grasses and foliage. Thus your movements would be slow, and it would be easy for the enemy to hide and unexpectedly move in on you. Sun Tzu suggests that you move quickly over the marshes and back yourself up to a clump of trees. Translating this tactic to your battle with the ego, if you find yourself vulnerable to attack by your ego, be sure to protect yourself.

How might you protect yourself from your ego's attacks? For example, do you eat when you find yourself upset? This action is likely another ploy by your ego to sabotage you by making you feel bad about yourself. How might you then protect yourself, knowing that doing so is a habit you have formed in response to stress or anxiety? One strategy might be to have healthy snack foods that you enjoy on hand, so that you can choose healthy eating. Find at least one protective strategy you can begin to practice when you find yourself vulnerable to your ego's attacks.

4. *#9: "In dry, level country, take up an easily accessible position with rising ground to your right and on your rear, so that the danger may be in front, and safety lie behind. So much for campaigning in flat country. #10: These are the four useful branches of military knowledge which enabled the Yellow Emperor to vanquish four several sovereigns."* It is important that you do not leave yourself vulnerable. Keeping the enemy directly in front of you protects you from unexpected attack. Write about a situation in which you left yourself open to attack. How can you avoid doing so in the future?

5. *#11: "All armies prefer high ground to low and sunny places to dark. #12: If you are careful of your men, and camp on hard ground, the army will be free from disease of every kind, and this will spell victory. #13: When you come to a hill or a bank, occupy the sunny side, with the slope on your right rear. Thus you will at once act for the benefit of your soldiers and utilize the natural advantages of the ground."* This tactic references freeing your army from disease. Emotional issues can take a toll on your physical health as well as your mental health. How has dis-ease shown up on your life? Do you believe it is

related to stressors that have been created by your ego? Explain.

6. #14: *"When, in consequence of heavy rains up-country, a river which you wish to ford is swollen and flecked with foam, you must wait until it subsides."* How often do you find yourself reacting to another, when you know you should step away from the situation until you become calm and level headed? Write about a situation in which you were reactive. What were the consequences? What might have happened had you not been reactive?

7. #15: *"Country in which there are precipitous cliffs with torrents running between, deep natural hollows, confined places, tangled thickets, quagmires and crevasses, should be left with all possible speed and not approached. #16: While we keep away from such places, we should get the enemy to approach them; while we face them, we should let the enemy have them on his rear. #17: If in the neighborhood of your camp there should be any hilly country, ponds surrounded by aquatic grass, hollow basins filled with reeds, or woods with thick undergrowth, they must be carefully routed out and searched; for these are places where men in ambush or insidious spies are likely to be lurking."* Again, it is important that you stay away from situations or people that could ambush you. Let's focus on your work environment. Are there individuals there that push your buttons and cause you frustration and anxiety? If so, what can you strategically do differently to protect yourself in the future. Write out some strategies you can use, and then try to practice them. Journal on your findings.

8. #18: *"When the enemy is close at hand and remains quiet, he is relying on the natural strength of his position. #19:*

When he keeps aloof and tries to provoke a battle, he is anxious for the other side to advance. #20: If his place of encampment is easy of access, he is tendering a bait." Your ego uses habit as part of its strategy. You are familiar with acting and reacting in a habitual way, so part of your strategy must be to break your ego's destructive habits. Focus on two habitual self-destructive behaviors that you perform. List them below and then make an effort to break free from the habit. Write about your findings.

9. #21: *"Movement amongst the trees of a forest shows that the enemy is advancing. The appearance of a number of screens in the midst of thick grass means that the enemy wants to make us suspicious. #22: The rising of birds in their flight is the sign of an ambuscade. Startled beasts indicate that a sudden attack is coming. #23: When there is dust rising in a high column, it is the sign of chariots advancing; when the dust is low, but spread over a wide area, it betokens the approach of infantry. When it branches out in different directions, it shows that parties have been sent to collect firewood. A few clouds of dust moving to and fro signify that the army is encamping."* Sun Tzu is very thorough in his observation of the environment that lends itself to attack. These warnings involve foresight in preparing for the enemy invasion. What signs do you receive that your ego is ready to attack? For example, do you find yourself short-tempered and reactive when you are tired and hungry? Do you find yourself to be extra critical when you near a work deadline? Do you easily anger when you haven't given yourself enough recreation time? Write a list of the "warning signs" that you need to note that often end in your ego's attack. Then note these signs as they arise, and take 1-minute and do some deep breathing, and quieting of your anxiety.

10. *#24: "Humble words and increased preparations are signs that the enemy is about to advance. Violent language and driving forward as if to the attack are signs that he will retreat. #25: When the light chariots come out first and take up a position on the wings, it is a sign that the enemy is forming for battle."* There is great wisdom in these observations. When you consider exchanges with others and ultimately within your own mind, what happens with your ego once you have heard "violent language"? Often others are venting, and their anger, while appearing to be about you, is always about themselves. If you can note that during the exchange, you will find that your energy will not be drained. Next time someone violently verbally attacks you, try repeating to yourself, *"This is not about me. This is not about me . . ."* Note how differently you feel about the attack. Do this as well when your critical mind attacks you. Note that it is attacking because it feels frightened and weak. Its attack is not about your true, higher self. It is your ego's efforts to remain powerful. In fact, it is evidence that your efforts are working to lessen its power over you. Congratulate yourself on your growing success!

11. *#26: "Peace proposals unaccompanied by a sworn covenant indicate a plot."* Contracts are necessary communiqués when trying to find resolution in battle. Take some time to write out a peace proposal with your ego. At the end of the treaty, create signature lines upon which both your wise-self and your ego should sign. When you feel full commitment to making peace with your ego, take time to re-read and sign it as a declaration and contract on your intention.

12. *#27: "When there is much running about and the soldiers fall into rank, it means that the critical moment has come. #28: "When some are seen advancing and some retreat-*

ing, it is a lure. #29: When the soldiers stand leaning on their spears, they are faint from want of food. #30: If those who are sent to draw water begin by drinking themselves, the army is suffering from thirst. #31: If the enemy sees an advantage to be gained and makes no effort to secure it, the soldiers are exhausted." These are all signs of potentially waning enemy forces. List any evidence you have that your ego is waning, and exhausting itself. Check this list and continue to add to it on a regular basis.

13. *#32: "If birds gather on any spot, it is unoccupied. Clamor by night betokens nervousness. #33: If there is disturbance in the camp, the general's authority is weak. If the banners and flags are shifted about, sedition is afoot. If the officers are angry, it means that the men are weary."* Note your sleeping habits. Has your sleep been disturbed since forging ahead in this battle? If so, find a quiet meditation or peaceful music to play prior to going to sleep. Focus on all that you are grateful for about your day as your drift off to sleep. If you awaken with a busy mind in the night, focus on your breathe and again, note all that you are grateful for in your life. This will quiet the enemy mind and build your sense of calm.

14. *#34: "When an army feeds its horses with grain and kills its cattle for food, and when the men do not hang their cooking-pots over the camp-fires, showing that they will not return to their tents, you may know that they are determined to fight to the death. #35: The sight of men whispering together in small knots or speaking in subdued tones points to disaffection amongst the rank and file."* What are the signs that your ego sends that it is willing to "fight to the death"? In what circumstances do you find it most defiant and disturbed?

15. *#36: "Too frequent rewards signify that the enemy is at the end of his resources; too many punishments betray a condition of dire distress."* These conditions warn of changes in the enemy's strategies. Have you noted any changes in your ego's initiatives? If so, note them.

16. *#37: "To begin by bluster, but afterwards to take fright at the enemy's numbers, shows a supreme lack of intelligence."* Do not lose hope when your ego seems overwhelmingly strong. Very often when you commit to something, the exact opposite begins to play out in your life. Some say it is the universe testing you to see just how committed you really are. Since committing to this battle, do you feel you are being testing be experiencing even more extreme challenges playing out in your life? Explain.

17. *#38: "When envoys are sent with compliments in their mouths, it is a sign that the enemy wishes for a truce."* Are you experiencing any evidence of a truce in your ego's response to your initiatives? If so, what are the signs?

18. *#39: "If the enemy's troops march up angrily and remain facing ours for a long time without either joining battle or taking themselves off again, the situation is one that demands great vigilance and circumspection. #40: "If our troops are no more in number than the enemy, that is amply sufficient; it only means that no direct attack can be made. What we can do is simply to concentrate all our available strength, keep a close watch on the enemy, and obtain reinforcements."* At this point in your battle strategy, list two additional reinforcements you could add to your initiatives. Some examples: you commit to meditating for 5 minutes each day to quiet your mind; you go for a quiet walk each day, focusing on being in the pres-

ent moment, enjoying nature; or you get a massage once each month as a de-stressor and a means of additional self-care and honoring of the work that you have been doing.

19. *#41: "He who exercises no forethought but makes light of his opponents is sure to be captured by them."* When have you "made light" of your ego's actions? What has been the result of doing so?

20. *#42: "If soldiers are punished before they have grown attached to you, they will not prove submissive; and, unless submissive, then will be practically useless. If, when the soldiers have become attached to you, punishments are not enforced, they will still be unless. #43: Therefore soldiers must be treated in the first instance with humanity, but kept under control by means of iron discipline. This is a certain road to victory."* These tenets speak of balancing care of your band of soldiers with iron-clad discipline. How has balance been played out in your life? Do you demonstrate enough self-care? Do you commit fully, without wavering? How much you improve upon your sense of balance as you continue on this battle?

21. *#44: "If in training soldiers commands are habitually enforced, the army will be well-disciplined; if not, its discipline will be bad. #45: "If a general shows confidence in his men but always insists on his orders being obeyed, the gain will be mutual."* These tenets again emphasize balance as being key to your strength. Do you have confidence in yourself? Do you have confidence in those that work with and for you? Are you able to delegate responsibilities to others, or do you burden yourself with doing menial things that a commander would not do, all

because you need to be in control Reflect on your ability or inability to delegate. Write about your findings, focusing on some key strategies you can put into practice that would improve upon your trust of others, and ultimately of yourself.

X.

Terrain

1. Sun Tzu said: We may distinguish six kinds of terrain, to wit:
     (1) Accessible ground;
     (2) entangling ground;
     (3) temporizing ground;
     (4) narrow passes;
     (5) precipitous heights;
     (6) positions at a great distance from the enemy.

2. Ground which can be freely traversed by both sides is called accessible.

3. With regard to ground of this nature, be before the enemy in occupying the raised and sunny spots, and carefully guard your line of supplies. Then you will be able to fight with advantage.

4. Ground which can be abandoned but is hard to re-occupy is called entangling.

5. From a position of this sort, if the enemy is unprepared, you may sally forth and defeat him. But if the enemy is prepared for your coming, and you fail to defeat him, then, return being impossible, disaster will ensue.

6. When the position is such that neither side will gain by making the first move, it is called temporizing ground.

7. In a position of this sort, even though the enemy should offer us an attractive bait, it will be advisable not to stir forth, but rather to retreat, thus enticing the enemy in his turn; then, when part of his army has come out, we may deliver our attack with advantage.

8. With regard to narrow passes, if you can occupy them first, let them be strongly garrisoned and await the advent of the enemy.

9. Should the army forestall you in occupying a pass, do not go after him if the pass is fully garrisoned, but only if it is weakly garrisoned.

10. With regard to precipitous heights, if you are beforehand with your adversary, you should occupy the raised and sunny spots, and there wait for him to come up.

11. If the enemy has occupied them before you, do not follow him, but retreat and try to entice him away.

12. If you are situated at a great distance from the enemy, and the strength of the two armies is equal, it is not easy to provoke a battle, and fighting will be to your disadvantage.

13. These six are the principles connected with Earth. The general who has attained a responsible post must be careful to study them.

14. Now an army is exposed to six several calamities, not arising from natural causes, but from faults for which the general is responsible. These are:
    (1) Flight;
    (2) insubordination;
    (3) collapse;
    (4) ruin;
    (5) disorganization;
    (6) rout.

15. Other conditions being equal, if one force is hurled against another ten times its size, the result will be the flight of the former.

16. When the common soldiers are too strong and their officers too weak, the result is insubordination. When the officers are too strong and the common soldiers too weak, the result is collapse.

17. When the higher officers are angry and insubordinate, and on meeting the enemy give battle on their own account from a feeling of resentment, before the commander-in-chief can tell whether or no he is in a position to fight, the result is ruin.

18. When the general is weak and without authority; when his orders are not clear and distinct; when there are no fixes duties assigned to officers and men, and the ranks are formed in a slovenly haphazard manner, the result is utter disorganization.

19. When a general, unable to estimate the enemy's strength, allows an inferior force to engage a larger one, or hurls a weak detachment against a powerful one, and neglects to place picked soldiers in the front rank, the result must be rout.

20. These are six ways of courting defeat, which must be carefully noted by the general who has attained a responsible post.

21. The natural formation of the country is the soldier's best ally; but a power of estimating the adversary, of controlling the forces of victory, and of shrewdly calculating difficulties, dangers and distances, constitutes the test of a great general.

22. He who knows these things, and in fighting puts his knowledge into practice, will win his battles.

He who knows them not, nor practices them, will surely be defeated.

23. If fighting is sure to result in victory, then you must fight, even though the ruler forbid it; if fighting will not result in victory, then you must not fight even at the ruler's bidding.

24. The general who advances without coveting fame and retreats without fearing disgrace, whose only thought is to protect his country and do good service for his sovereign, is the jewel of the kingdom.

25. Regard your soldiers as your children, and they will follow you into the deepest valleys; look upon them as your own beloved sons, and they will stand by you even unto death.

26. If, however, you are indulgent, but unable to make your authority felt; kind-hearted, but unable to enforce your commands; and incapable, moreover, of quelling disorder: then your soldiers must be likened to spoilt children; they are useless for any practical purpose.

27. If we know that our own men are in a condition to attack, but are unaware that the enemy is not open to attack, we have gone only halfway towards victory.

28. If we know that the enemy is open to attack, but are unaware that our own men are not in a condition to attack, we have gone only halfway towards victory.

29. If we know that the enemy is open to attack, and also know that our men are in a condition to attack, but are unaware that the nature of the ground makes fighting impracticable, we have still gone only halfway towards victory.

30. Hence the experienced soldier, once in motion, is never bewildered; once he has broken camp, he is never at a loss.

31. Hence the saying: If you know the enemy and know yourself, your victory will not stand in doubt; if you know Heaven and know Earth, you may make your victory complete.

X. Terrain

In this chapter Sun Tzu gets very specific about the six kinds of terrain upon which you would fight, along with the six potential calamities that could befall you and your army. The six terrain each map out challenges you likely face with your ego. Having foresight on what those challenges may be, as well as having a master plan that would aptly respond to calamities sets you in a stronger position against your flailing ego.

1. *#1: "Sun Tzu said: We may distinguish six kinds of terrain, to wit: (1) Accessible ground; (2) entangling ground; (3) temporizing ground; (4) narrow passes; (5) precipitous heights; (6) positions at a great distance from the enemy. #13: These six are the challenges one faces connected with Earth. The general who has attained a responsible post must be careful to study them."* You could liken these six terrains to the six environmental conditions that affect the playing field in which you do battle with your ego. Here is an overview of each of these states: 1) Accessible ground: When the face of your ego is fully exposed and unprotected. 2) Entangled ground: Situations in which the parts of your ego that you thought you had left behind or done away with may arise. (3) Temporizing ground: When you find yourself paralyzed and unable to move through a situation. (4) Narrow passes: Situations in which there is little room for alternative responses. (5) Precipitous

heights: Situations in which you have reached apparent vast heights. (6) Positions at a great distance from the enemy: Situations in which eventual conflict will arise, but is not imminent.

2. #2: *"Ground which can be freely traversed by both sides is called accessible. #3: With regard to ground of this nature, be before the enemy in occupying the raised and sunny spots, and carefully guard your line of supplies. Then you will be able to fight with advantage."* To reiterate, 1) Accessible ground: When the face of your ego is fully exposed and unprotected. In situations in which your ego's acting out is obvious, to gain the upper hand, it is best that whenever possible, you anticipate your ego's arrival and expected behavior. Sometimes calling it out is the best tactic. For example, if you note a co-worked is being praised for doing exceptional work, and you feel inferior and jealous, as opposed to having the jealousy fester and grow inside of you, approach the co-worker and congratulate him/her for his/her prowess. If you are a bold warrior, you could even claim your jealousy with, *"Hey, buddy. You really did an awesome job on that presentation. Heck, I'm jealous. Nice work!"* Try this tactic next time you find your ego exposed. Write about your findings.

3. #4: *"Ground which can be abandoned but is hard to re-occupy is called entangling. #5: "From a position of this sort, if the enemy is unprepared, you may sally forth and defeat him. But if the enemy is prepared for your coming, and you fail to defeat him, then, return being impossible, disaster will ensue."* Again, 2) Entangled ground involves situations in which the parts of your ego that you thought you had left behind or done away with may arise. Examples of these environmental challenges might be seeing

an old friend that you no longer befriended at a reunion. You had made a conscious choice to leave the friendship because it was not healthy for you, but unbeknownst to you, that ex-friend was at the same event. Being in their presence inflames your ego. In such situations, it may be best to be polite, but not necessarily engage with the individual again. There was a reason that you originally ended the friendship, and resurrecting it again would likely be defeat. Have you ever found yourself in such as situation? If so, how did you handle it? With the new knowledge you have about your ego, would you do anything differently?

4. #6: *"When the position is such that neither side will gain by making the first move, it is called temporizing ground. #7: In a position of this sort, even though the enemy should offer us an attractive bait, it will be advisable not to stir forth, but rather to retreat, thus enticing the enemy in his turn; then, when part of his army has come out, we may deliver our attack with advantage."* 3) Temporizing ground: When you find yourself paralyzed and unable to move through a situation. Have you ever found yourself paralyzed and feeling a sense of hopelessness and helplessness in a situation? If you catch yourself in self-criticism, hearing your ego state, "You should take action", note that the word "should" is often a trigger and trick. Take care to make choices from the place of confidence and desire, not guilt. Make a list of the actions that you take because you "should" do them. Then review the list, and ascertain whether or not the action truly benefits you and those around you. If it does not, you may want to cease it.

5. #8: *"With regard to narrow passes, if you can occupy them first, let them be strongly garrisoned and await the*

advent of the enemy. #9: Should the army forestall you in occupying a pass, do not go after him if the pass is fully garrisoned, but only if it is weakly garrisoned." (4) Narrow passes: Situations in which there is little room for alternative responses. Have you found yourself in very tight situations, where you had little room to maneuver yourself out of? For example, you have tight schedule where you have to rush to a designated bus from the train in order to get to work on time. This environmental stressor leaves you little room to de-stress and often creates anxiety that can overwhelm you and allow your ego to prevail. What action steps could you take to alleviate your anxiety in such situations? In this case, you might find five minutes either during the bus route or once you arrive at work to decompress (meditate, do some deep breathing, listen to music that calms and inspires you, etc. Write about a similar situation that you often find yourself in, finding ways to de-compress.

6. *#10: "With regard to precipitous heights, if you are beforehand with your adversary, you should occupy the raised and sunny spots, and there wait for him to come up. #11: "If the enemy has occupied them before you, do not follow him, but retreat and try to entice him away."* (5) Precipitous heights: Situations in which you have reached apparent vast heights. Your ego can also play tricks on you once you have tasted victory. It has a way of inflaming itself, being arrogant and claiming the victory as a personal feat. This can alienate others and keep you from experience humility and deep gratitude. Write about a situation in which your lack of humility has affected you. What was the outcome?

7. *#12: "If you are situated at a great distance from the enemy, and the strength of the two armies is equal, it is*

not easy to provoke a battle, and fighting will be to your disadvantage." (6) Positions at a great distance from the enemy: Situations in which eventual conflict will arise, but is not imminent. You must keep your ego's musings close at hand. Again, as you start to achieve victory, you could lose sight of its trickery. Imagine yourself victorious, feeling peaceful and content. Imagine the ways that your ego can intervene. List them.

8. *#14: "Now an army is exposed to six several calamities, not arising from natural causes, but from faults for which the general is responsible. These are:*
   (1) Flight;
   (2) insubordination;
   (3) collapse;
   (4) ruin;
   (5) disorganization;
   (6) rout."

These conditions are not natural, but occur when the general does not effectively command his army. Provide examples of how your ego demonstrates each of these "calamities:

   (1) Flight (when avoided dealing with an issue/close down):

   (2) Insubordination (when you intentionally behave disrespectfully towards yourself or others):

   (3) Collapse (when you felt paralyzed, like everything has fallen apart):

   (4) Ruin (the end of segment of your life—losing a job, dear one, etc.):

   (5) Disorganization (when you experience great confusion that clouds clarity):

   (6) Rout (when everything and everyone around you seems against you):

9. *#15: "Other conditions being equal, if one force is hurled against another ten times its size, the result will be the flight of the former."* One force has much less strength than force ten times it size, even when hurled against them. Often when we passionate react against something, the strength of that reaction may weaken us. For example, if you react very defensively and strongly against someone else's criticism, in some way you believe their assertion. If you did not believe it, you would not react so strongly. Think of potent situation when a criticism was hurled at you, and really hurt you. In retrospect was there a part of you that questioned yourself? Write about your findings.

10. *#16: "When the common soldiers are too strong and their officers too weak, the result is insubordination. When the officers are too strong and the common soldiers too weak, the result is collapse."* This tenet is about balance of your forces in battle. If you see the officers as the visionary, and the soldiers as the follow through, it is important to balance your intentions with your actions. If you are a visionary in your life, but you do not follow through, you will lose energy. The inaction is the result of the ego. Do you ever find yourself getting enthusiastic about innovations or ideas and then find yourself wanting to move forward with them, but you do not? Write about ideas, insights and innovations with which you did not move forward.

11. *#17: "When the higher officers are angry and insubordinate, and on meeting the enemy give battle on their own account from a feeling of resentment, before the commander-in-chief can tell whether or no he is in a position to fight, the result is ruin."* Resentment feeds power to your ego. Write a list of the people you resent in your life. Then write why you resent each of them. After doing

this, reflect on each, asking yourself whether or not holding onto that resentment is worth being beaten by your ego. Be careful not to force yourself to forgive those you resent, but reflect and at least set an intention to heal your anger.

12. #18: *"When the general is weak and without authority; when his orders are not clear and distinct; when there are no fixes duties assigned to officers and men, and the ranks are formed in a slovenly haphazard manner, the result is utter disorganization."* Are you clear about the steps you need to take in your battle? Revisit and review them. Write them down in an orderly fashion.

13. #19: *"When a general, unable to estimate the enemy's strength, allows an inferior force to engage a larger one, or hurls a weak detachment against a powerful one, and neglects to place picked soldiers in the front rank, the result must be rout. #20: "These are six ways of courting defeat, which must be carefully noted by the general who has attained a responsible post."* You need to be aware of the strength of your ego. On a scale from one to ten (one being "poor" and ten being "excellent"), rate how powerful you believe your ego to be.

1———2———3———4———5———6———7———8———9———10

14. #21: *"The natural formation of the country is the soldier's best ally; but a power of estimating the adversary, of controlling the forces of victory, and of shrewdly calculating difficulties, dangers and distances, constitutes the test of a great general. #22: He who knows these things, and in fighting puts his knowledge into practice, will win his battles. He who knows them not, nor practices them, will surely be defeated."* These tenets deal with being prepared and anticipating the unexpected. On a scale from

one to ten (one being "poor" and ten being "excellent"), rate how good you are when faced with unexpected challenges.

1———2———3———4———5———6———7———8———9———10

15. #23: *"If fighting is sure to result in victory, then you must fight, even though the ruler forbid it; if fighting will not result in victory, then you must not fight even at the ruler's bidding."* This tenet points out that victory is key, whatever the bidding of ruler might be. Sometimes others have their own agenda. If you fight your ego, you affect their world. Sometimes others may even resent you when you change yourself for the better. Have you noted anyone being disturbed about your efforts to find more peace in your life? If so, who? Why do you think they are not happy with your efforts?

16. #24: *"The general who advances without coveting fame and retreats without fearing disgrace, whose only thought is to protect his country and do good service for his sovereign, is the jewel of the kingdom. #25: Regard your soldiers as your children, and they will follow you into the deepest valleys; look upon them as your own beloved sons, and they will stand by you even unto death."* Both of these tenets emphasize the power of a general who is altruistic and fights for the greater good of all. List the ways in which you are honorable in your efforts, and don't hesitate to note all that you do right in your efforts.

17. #26: *"If, however, you are indulgent, but unable to make your authority felt; kind-hearted, but unable to enforce your commands; and incapable, moreover, of quelling disorder: then your soldiers must be likened to spoilt children; they are useless for any practical purpose."* Do you forgive your laziness, procrastinations or avoidances too

easily, without making yourself accountable? If so, who might you call on to assist you in being held accountable to your commitments. Write the names of at least 2 people you could count on. Then approach at least one of them, explaining what you are doing and why you need his/her support.

18. *#27: "If we know that our own men are in a condition to attack, but are unaware that the enemy is not open to attack, we have gone only halfway towards victory. #28: "If we know that the enemy is open to attack, but are unaware that our own men are not in a condition to attack, we have gone only halfway towards victory. #29: If we know that the enemy is open to attack, and also know that our men are in a condition to attack, but are unaware that the nature of the ground makes fighting impracticable, we have still gone only halfway towards victory. #30: Hence the experienced soldier, once in motion, is never bewildered; once he has broken camp, he is never at a loss. #31: Hence the saying: If you know the enemy and know yourself, your victory will not stand in doubt; if you know Heaven and know Earth, you may make your victory complete."* These tenets hold true that you need to always be really and aware of your surroundings when fighting the enemy ego. You have "broken camp", thus everything you have done until now is not in vain. You must know this, and understand that you are participating in the battle and that you are moving forward. Write a letter of gratitude to yourself for the powerful and courageous work that you are doing. Read it aloud to yourself.

XI.

The Nine Situations

1. Sun Tzu said: The art of war recognizes nine varieties of ground:
   (1) Dispersive ground;
   (2) facile ground;
   (3) contentious ground;
   (4) open ground;
   (5) ground of intersecting highways;
   (6) serious ground;
   (7) difficult ground;
   (8) hemmed-in ground;
   (9) desperate ground.

2. When a chieftain is fighting in his own territory, it is dispersive ground.

3. When he has penetrated into hostile territory, but to no great distance, it is facile ground.

4. Ground the possession of which imports great advantage to either side, is contentious ground.

5. Ground on which each side has liberty of movement is open ground.

6. Ground which forms the key to three contiguous states, so that he who occupies it first has most of the Empire at his command, is a ground of intersecting highways.

7. When an army has penetrated into the heart of a hostile country, leaving a number of fortified cities in its rear, it is serious ground.

8. Mountain forests, rugged steeps, marshes and fens—all country that is hard to traverse: this is difficult ground.

9. Ground which is reached through narrow gorges, and from which we can only retire by tortuous paths, so that a small number of the enemy would suffice to crush a large body of our men: this is hemmed in ground.

10. Ground on which we can only be saved from destruction by fighting without delay, is desperate ground.

11. On dispersive ground, therefore, fight not. On facile ground, halt not. On contentious ground, attack not.

12. On open ground, do not try to block the enemy's way. On the ground of intersecting highways, join hands with your allies.

13. On serious ground, gather in plunder. In difficult ground, keep steadily on the march.

14. On hemmed-in ground, resort to stratagem. On desperate ground, fight.

15. Those who were called skillful leaders of old knew how to drive a wedge between the enemy's front and rear; to prevent co-operation between his large and small divisions; to hinder the good troops from rescuing the bad, the officers from rallying their men.

16. When the enemy's men were united, they managed to keep them in disorder.

17. When it was to their advantage, they made a forward move; when otherwise, they stopped still.

18. If asked how to cope with a great host of the enemy in orderly array and on the point of marching to the attack, I should say: "Begin by seizing something which your opponent holds dear; then he will be amenable to your will."

19. Rapidity is the essence of war: take advantage of the enemy's unreadiness, make your way by unexpected routes, and attack unguarded spots.

20. The following are the principles to be observed by an invading force: The further you penetrate into a country, the greater will be the solidarity of your troops, and thus the defenders will not prevail against you.

21. Make forays in fertile country in order to supply your army with food.

22. Carefully study the well-being of your men, and do not overtax them. Concentrate your energy and hoard your strength. Keep your army continually on the move, and devise unfathomable plans.

23. Throw your soldiers into positions whence there is no escape, and they will prefer death to flight. If they will face death, there is nothing they may not achieve. Officers and men alike will put forth their uttermost strength.

24. Soldiers when in desperate straits lose the sense of fear. If there is no place of refuge, they will stand firm. If they are in hostile country, they will show a stubborn front. If there is no help for it, they will fight hard.

25. Thus, without waiting to be marshaled, the soldiers will be constantly on the qui vive; without waiting to be asked, they will do your will; without restrictions, they will be faithful; without giving orders, they can be trusted.

26. Prohibit the taking of omens, and do away with superstitious doubts. Then, until death itself comes, no calamity need be feared.

27. If our soldiers are not overburdened with money, it is not because they have a distaste for riches; if their lives are not unduly long, it is not because they are disinclined to longevity.

28. On the day they are ordered out to battle, your soldiers may weep, those sitting up bedewing their garments, and those lying down letting the tears run down their cheeks. But let them once be brought to bay, and they will display the courage of a Chu or a Kuei.

29. The skillful tactician may be likened to the shuai-jan. Now the shuai-jan is a snake that is found in the ChUng mountains. Strike at its head, and you will be attacked by its tail; strike at its tail, and you will be attacked by its head; strike at its middle, and you will be attacked by head and tail both.

30. Asked if an army can be made to imitate the shuai-jan, I should answer, Yes. For the men of Wu and the men of Yueh are enemies; yet if they are crossing a river in the same boat and are caught by a storm, they will come to each other's assistance just as the left hand helps the right.

31. Hence it is not enough to put one's trust in the tethering of horses, and the burying of chariot wheels in the ground

32. The principle on which to manage an army is to set up one standard of courage which all must reach.

33. How to make the best of both strong and weak— that is a question involving the proper use of ground.

34. Thus the skillful general conducts his army just as though he were leading a single man, willy-nilly, by the hand.

35. It is the business of a general to be quiet and thus ensure secrecy; upright and just, and thus maintain order.

36. He must be able to mystify his officers and men by false reports and appearances, and thus keep them in total ignorance.

37. By altering his arrangements and changing his plans, he keeps the enemy without definite knowledge. By shifting his camp and taking circuitous routes, he prevents the enemy from anticipating his purpose.

38. At the critical moment, the leader of an army acts like one who has climbed up a height and then kicks away the ladder behind him. He carries his men deep into hostile territory before he shows his hand.

39. He burns his boats and breaks his cooking-pots; like a shepherd driving a flock of sheep, he drives his men this way and that, and nothing knows whither he is going.

40. To muster his host and bring it into danger: this may be termed the business of the general.

41. The different measures suited to the nine varieties of ground; the expediency of aggressive or defensive tactics; and the fundamental laws of human nature: these are things that must most certainly be studied.

42. When invading hostile territory, the general principle is, that penetrating deeply brings cohesion; penetrating but a short way means dispersion.

43. When you leave your own country behind, and take your army across neighborhood territory, you find yourself on critical ground. When there are means of communication on all four sides, the ground is one of intersecting highways.

44. When you penetrate deeply into a country, it is serious ground. When you penetrate but a little way, it is facile ground.

45. When you have the enemy's strongholds on your rear, and narrow passes in front, it is hemmed- in ground. When there is no place of refuge at all, it is desperate ground.

46. Therefore, on dispersive ground, I would inspire my men with unity of purpose. On facile ground, I would see that there is close connection between all parts of my army.

47. On contentious ground, I would hurry up my rear.

48. On open ground, I would keep a vigilant eye on my defenses. On ground of intersecting highways, I would consolidate my alliances.

49. On serious ground, I would try to ensure a continuous stream of supplies. On difficult ground, I would keep pushing on along the road.

50. On hemmed-in ground, I would block any way of retreat. On desperate ground, I would proclaim to my soldiers the hopelessness of saving their lives.

51. For it is the soldier's disposition to offer an obstinate resistance when surrounded, to fight hard when he cannot help himself, and to obey promptly when he has fallen into danger.

52. We cannot enter into alliance with neighboring princes until we are acquainted with their designs. We are not fit to lead an army on the march unless we are familiar with the face of the country—its mountains and forests, its pitfalls and precipices, its marshes and swamps. We shall be unable to turn natural advantages to account unless we make use of local guides.

53. To be ignored of any one of the following four or five principles does not befit a warlike prince.

54. When a warlike prince attacks a powerful state, his generalship shows itself in preventing the concentration of the enemy's forces. He overawes his opponents, and their allies are prevented from joining against him.

55. Hence he does not strive to ally himself with all and sundry, nor does he foster the power of other states.

He carries out his own secret designs, keeping his antagonists in awe. Thus he is able to capture their cities and overthrow their kingdoms.

56. Bestow rewards without regard to rule, issue orders without regard to previous arrangements; and you will be able to handle a whole army as though you had to do with but a single man.

57. Confront your soldiers with the deed itself; never let them know your design. When the outlook is bright, bring it before their eyes; but tell them nothing when the situation is gloomy.

58. Place your army in deadly peril, and it will survive; plunge it into desperate straits, and it will come off in safety.

59. For it is precisely when a force has fallen into harm's way that is capable of striking a blow for victory.

60. Success in warfare is gained by carefully accommodating ourselves to the enemy's purpose.

61. By persistently hanging on the enemy's flank, we shall succeed in the long run in killing the commander-in-chief.

62. This is called ability to accomplish a thing by sheer cunning.

63. On the day that you take up your command, block the frontier passes, destroy the official tallies, and stop the passage of all emissaries.

64. Be stern in the council-chamber, so that you may control the situation.

65. If the enemy leaves a door open, you must rush in.

66. Forestall your opponent by seizing what he holds dear, and subtly contrive to time his arrival on the ground.

67. Walk in the path defined by rule, and accommodate yourself to the enemy until you can fight a decisive battle.

68. At first, then, exhibit the coyness of a maiden, until the enemy gives you an opening; afterwards emulate the rapidity of a running hare, and it will be too late for the enemy to oppose you.

STUDY GUIDE

XI. The Nine Situations

In this chapter, The Nine Situations, Sun Tzu maps out nine specific situations that you and your soldiers could come up against once you meet your enemy army. It is clear in these teachings that wisdom, forethought and power versus force all provide you with the insights, strength and energy to be a formidable foe in your battle against your ego.

1. #1: *"Sun Tzu said: The art of war recognizes nine varieties of ground: (1) Dispersive ground; (2) facile ground; (3) contentious ground; (4) open ground; (5) ground of intersecting highways; (6) serious ground; (7) difficult ground; (8) hemmed-in ground; (9) desperate ground."* To be able to win over your ego, the more you know about the terrain in which it flourishes, the better your chances of success will be when in combat with it. In which situations does your ego most wreak havoc in your life? Find a pattern of people or situations that trigger it most, and write about it in as much detail as possible.

2. #2: *"When a chieftain is fighting in his own territory, it is dispersive ground. #3. When he has penetrated into hostile territory, but to no great distance, it is facile ground. #4: Ground the possession of which imports great advantage to either side, is contentious ground. #5. Ground on which each side has liberty of movement is open ground. #6: Ground which forms the key to three contiguous*

states, so that he who occupies it first has most of the Empire at his command, is a ground of intersecting highways. #7: When an army has penetrated into the heart of a hostile country, leaving a number of fortified cities in its rear, it is serious ground. #8: Mountain forests, rugged steeps, marshes and fens—all country that is hard to traverse: this is difficult ground. #9: Ground which is reached through narrow gorges, and from which we can only retire by tortuous paths, so that a small number of the enemy would suffice to crush a large body of our men: this is hemmed in ground. #10: Ground on which we can only be saved from destruction by fighting without delay, is desperate ground." Reflect on the situation you referenced in the previous question. Based on these descriptions of the various terrains, upon which ground is this battle being fought upon. How vulnerable is your ego, compared to your highest self?

3. #11: "On dispersive ground, therefore, fight not. On facile ground, halt not. On contentious ground, attack not." If you can "witness" your ego at work when it hasn't yet made "great distance" in a pending upsetting situation, you have a chance to change its behavior. Throughout the next day, really focus on witnessing your ego at work. When you see it being triggered, blast it with nonjudgment and compassion. Talk it down, so to speak, listening to the message it is trying to convey. Doing so will often ease it into feeling safer and calmer Write about your experience.

4. #12: "On open ground, do not try to block the enemy's way. On the ground of intersecting highways, join hands with your allies." Often when your life is at a crossroads (a point at which you may be preparing for something new situations), your ego will especially act out because of

fear of change. In which areas of your life do you believe you are currently at a crossroad? Is your ego responding to the imminent change(s)? If so, how? What might you do to calm the ego's fears?

5. *#13: "On serious ground, gather in plunder. In difficult ground, keep steadily on the march. #14: On hemmed-in ground, resort to stratagem. On desperate ground, fight."* In what situations do you think you have mastered command over your ego? List at least two situations in which you were able to keep your ego from hurting you or others through judgment, defensiveness, contempt, numbing, raging or other sabotaging behaviors.

6. *#15: "Those who were called skillful leaders of old knew how to drive a wedge between the enemy's front and rear; to prevent co-operation between his large and small divisions; to hinder the good troops from rescuing the bad, the officers from rallying their men. #16: "When the enemy's men were united, they managed to keep them in disorder. #17: "When it was to their advantage, they made a forward move; when otherwise, they stopped still."* In what ways does the "skillful leader" within you show up in your life? Where do you flourish as a leader of men and women? Explain.

7. *#18: If asked how to cope with a great host of the enemy in orderly array and on the point of marching to the attack, I should say: "Begin by seizing something which your opponent holds dear; then he will be amenable to your will."* What does your ego "hold dear" that you could use to strategically gain the upper hand in your battles with it? How might you do so?

8. *#19: "Rapidity is the essence of war: take advantage of the enemy's unreadiness, make your way by unexpected*

routes, and attack unguarded spots." How well do you believe you handle having to move fast, with little or no preparation time? On a scale from one to ten (one being "poor" and ten being "excellent"), rate how well you handle unanticipated surprises when they arrive.

9. *#20: "The following are the principles to be observed by an invading force: The further you penetrate into a country, the greater will be the solidarity of your troops, and thus the defenders will not prevail against you. #21: Make forays in fertile country in order to supply your army with food."* The more fully committed you are to attaining inner peace, the greater your strength and the solidarity behind your highest self. Create a depiction of your life as you experience greater inner peace. Draw a picture, or make a collage using photos or magazine clipping that reflect the greater well being you will feel. Then put the depiction in a place where you can frequently view it. This will feed your sense of hope in achieving your desired goals.

10. *#22: "Carefully study the well-being of your men, and do not overtax them. Concentrate your energy and hoard your strength. Keep your army continually on the move, and devise unfathomable plans."* Maintaining physical strength in supporting your emotional efforts is very important. On a scale from one to ten (one being "not at all" and ten being "very fit"), you're your current state of physical fitness.

11. What steps can you immediately take to improve upon your overall health? Write a plan and begin putting it into practice.

12. *#23: "Throw your soldiers into positions whence there is no escape, and they will prefer death to flight. If they will face death, there is nothing they may not achieve. Officers and men alike will put forth their uttermost strength. #24: "Soldiers when in desperate straits lose the sense of fear. If there is no place of refuge, they will stand firm. If they are in hostile country, they will show a stubborn front. If there is no help for it, they will fight hard. #25: Thus, without waiting to be marshaled, the soldiers will be constantly on the qui vive; without waiting to be asked, they will do your will; without restrictions, they will be faithful; without giving orders, they can be trusted."* What would have to happen in your life to create such a powerful force against further heartache, confusion and chaos in dealing with your ego? Imagine you were told that you had one week left to live on this earth. You have been advised to say goodbye to your loved ones, and make amends with your enemies. Close your eyes and imagine such a scene. What steps would you take to get things in order prior to leaving? After imagining, write a "to do" list. Then reflect on the list, and see what you might be inspired to do at this time in your life.

13. *#26: "Prohibit the taking of omens, and do away with superstitious doubts. Then, until death itself comes, no calamity need be feared."* Are you superstitious? If so, does the superstition serve your highest good or your ego? If your ego, are you willing to let it go?

14. *#27: "If our soldiers are not overburdened with money, it is not because they have a distaste for riches; if their lives are not unduly long, it is not because they are disinclined to longevity. #28: On the day they are ordered out to battle, your soldiers may weep, those sitting up bedewing their garments, and those lying down letting the tears*

run down their cheeks. But let them once be brought to bay, and they will display the courage of a Chu or a Kuei." In this principle, Sun Tzu references the variety of backgrounds that your soldiers may have. In the end, however, whatever their background, ultimately when faced with warfare, they will show great courage. What courageous act have you done of which you are most proud? Write about it, detailing why you are proud.

15. #29: *"The skillful tactician may be likened to the shuai-jan. Now the shuai-jan is a snake that is found in the ChUng mountains. Strike at its head, and you will be attacked by its tail; strike at its tail, and you will be attacked by its head; strike at its middle, and you will be attacked by head and tail both.#30. "Asked if an army can be made to imitate the shuai-jan, I should answer, Yes. For the men of Wu and the men of Yueh are enemies; yet if they are crossing a river in the same boat and are caught by a storm, they will come to each other's assistance just as the left hand helps the right."* This tenet encourages you to be prepared for attack from your ego on all sides and in all ways. It emphasizes, however, that when faced with a storm, the warring armies would protect and support one another. Thus, a sense of both courage and honor are noted and praised. Consider the individual that you struggle most with as the other army in the boat. Could you support him or her if he/she was in imminent danger? Have you ever assisted someone you consider your "enemy" when they were in need. Write about it. If not, write about situations in which you think you could assist and "enemy".

16. #31: *"Hence it is not enough to put one's trust in the tethering of horses, and the burying of chariot wheels in the ground. #32: "The principle on which to manage*

an army is to set up one standard of courage which all must reach." Building a strong army requires courage and strength in all of your soldiers. Check in with yourself at this time. Are there any parts of you that are feeling discouraged, tired or beaten? If so, which and how can you revived energy and hope into them?

17. #33: "*How to make the best of both strong and weak—that is a question involving the proper use of ground. #34: "Thus the skillful general conducts his army just as though he were leading a single man, willy-nilly, by the hand.*" You could see various times in your life as a variety of soldiers. You early childhood self cares issues and fears, as does your teenage self, and so forth. Taking them by the hand involved understanding them—knowing what issues have not been sufficiently dealt with and are affecting your present day judgment and behavior. Write a list of the emotional, physical and/or spiritual traumas you dealt with throughout your life. Reflect on whether any of them still affect your current life.

18. #35: "*It is the business of a general to be quiet and thus ensure secrecy; upright and just, and thus maintain order. #36: He must be able to mystify his officers and men by false reports and appearances, and thus keep them in total ignorance. #37: By altering his arrangements and changing his plans, he keeps the enemy without definite knowledge. By shifting his camp and taking circuitous routes, he prevents the enemy from anticipating his purpose.*" These principles reference tricking the enemy soldiers; keeping them unaware of your strategies. How does this play into your battle with your ego? Perhaps you have to be willing to forge ahead without always seeing clearly what your next step would be. Sometimes when you are committed to listening to your highest self, syn-

chronicities can begin to occur. When they do, you have to be aware of them and ready to take action. An example, you are struggling with painful grief you are experiencing at the loss of a loved one. Out of the blue, a friend mentions that they will be attending a Grief workshop in a couple of weeks. As it turns out, you had an appointment that conflicted, but it was cancelled. You note the workshop, and register for it. Taking action when opportunities present themselves can assist you in a speedy and easy victory. Write about a synchronistic situation that you experienced in your life. If you cannot think of one, anticipate and focus on having one show up in your life. Remain attentive and open.

19. *#38: "At the critical moment, the leader of an army acts like one who has climbed up a height and then kicks away the ladder behind him. He carries his men deep into hostile territory before he shows his hand. #39: He burns his boats and breaks his cooking-pots; like a shepherd driving a flock of sheep, he drives his men this way and that, and nothing knows whither he is going. #40: To muster his host and bring it into danger: this may be termed the business of the general."* To successfully command your army, you must have great courage and be willing to take away the safety nets as well. What "safety nets" are you still holding onto (perhaps relationships that no longer support you, food, living in the security of your childhood home, etc.)? Are they impeding upon your personal growth in any way? If so, can you let them go?

20. *#41: "The different measures suited to the nine varieties of ground; the expediency of aggressive or defensive tactics; and the fundamental laws of human nature: these are things that must most certainly be studied. #42: "When invading hostile territory, the general principle is,*

that penetrating deeply brings cohesion; penetrating but a short way means dispersion. #43" "When you leave your own country behind, and take your army across neighbor-hood territory, you find yourself on critical ground. When there are means of communication on all four sides, the ground is one of intersecting highways. #44: "When you penetrate deeply into a country, it is serious ground. When you penetrate but a little way, it is facile ground. #45: "When you have the enemy's strongholds on your rear, and narrow passes in front, it is hemmed-in ground. When there is no place of refuge at all, it is desperate ground. #46. "Therefore, on dispersive ground, I would inspire my men with unity of purpose. On facile ground, I would see that there is close connection between all parts of my army. #47: "On contentious ground, I would hurry up my rear. #48: On open ground, I would keep a vigilant eye on my defenses. On ground of intersecting highways, I would consolidate my alliances.#49. On seri-ous ground, I would try to ensure a continuous stream of supplies. On difficult ground, I would keep pushing on along the road. #50: On hemmed-in ground, I would block any way of retreat. On desperate ground, I would proclaim to my soldiers the hopelessness of saving their lives.#51: "For it is the soldier's disposition to offer an obstinate resistance when surrounded, to fight hard when he cannot help himself, and to obey promptly when he has fallen into danger." These tenets are very specific and detailed. A good commander has hundreds of strat-egies ready in his mind. She has practiced and imagined them so often that they become second nature. Have some of your negative responses to life become second nature? For example, do you watch what you say and how you say it? Do you often by habit say things like, *"That just kills me. I hate. . . , I'm dying to . . ."*? For the next week, focus on what you say. Note if you are negative or affirming in what you say and the way that you say it. When you catch yourself saying something negative, immediate state the opposite positive and affirming comment. For example, *"I hate the cold and snow"* could be changed to *"I look forward to plenty of warmth and sunshine."* Write down any negative comments you catch yourself saying, and then, just like in the example, write the related affirming positive statement.

21. *#52: "We cannot enter into alliance with neighboring princes until we are acquainted with their designs. We are not fit to lead an army on the march unless we are familiar with the face of the country—its mountains and forests, its pitfalls and precipices, its marshes and swamps. We shall be unable to turn natural advantages to account unless we make use of local guides."* Are there "neighboring princes" that you would like to be in alliance with; individuals who you respect and look up to? Perhaps there is someone who is highly successful that would like to be your mentor. Who might that be? Consider asking him or her for guidance. Write about your experience doing so.

22. *#53: "To be ignored of any one of the following four or five principles does not befit a warlike prince. #54: "When a warlike prince attacks a powerful state, his generalship shows itself in preventing the concentration of the enemy's forces. He overawes his opponents, and their allies are prevented from joining against him. #55: Hence he does not strive to ally himself with all and sundry, nor does he foster the power of other states. He carries out his own secret designs, keeping his antagonists in awe. Thus he is able to capture their cities and overthrow their kingdoms."* Write about a situation in which you "over-

awed" potential enemy forces in your life, turning enemies into allies.

23. #56: *"Bestow rewards without regard to rule, issue orders without regard to previous arrangements; and you will be able to handle a whole army as though you had to do with but a single man."* This tenet encourages you to have confidence in your abilities. When you are confident, you can move the most difficult of men. In what areas of your life do you feel most confident? In what areas would you like to cultivate greater confidence?

24. #57. *"Confront your soldiers with the deed itself; never let them know your design. When the outlook is bright, bring it before their eyes; but tell them nothing when the situation is gloomy.* #58: *"Place your army in deadly peril, and it will survive; plunge it into desperate straits, and it will come off in safety.* #59: *"For it is precisely when a force has fallen into harm's way that is capable of striking a blow for victory."* How much of your attention are you focusing on what you don't want in your life, as opposed to what you "do" want? Spend a great deal more time focusing on "when the outlook is bright" and you will experience more of that. For the next day, try spending every conscious moment focusing on what is working in your life; what you appreciate. Note how you feel by choosing to focus on what is working. Write about your experience

25. #60: *Success in warfare is gained by carefully accommodating ourselves to the enemy's purpose.* #61: *"By persistently hanging on the enemy's flank, we shall succeed in the long run in killing the commander-in-chief.* #62: *This is called ability to accomplish a thing by sheer cunning."* Where do you most display your cunning? Are you most effective working with different kinds of people, are you a

visionary, or excellent at following through on tasks? List the skills that you are most proficient at. Then write about how each has supported you in your battle against your ego's attacks.

26. #63: "On the day that you take up your command, block the frontier passes, destroy the official tallies, and stop the passage of all emissaries. #64. "Be stern in the council-chamber, so that you may control the situation. #65: "If the enemy leaves a door open, you must rush in." Does anyone else ever try to take command over you, thinking that they know better what is best for you? How do you handle them? Do you ever doubt yourself because of their strong conviction? What can you do in future to strengthen your own sense of self when they do?

27. #66: "Forestall your opponent by seizing what he holds dear, and subtly contrive to time his arrival on the ground." #67: "Walk in the path defined by rule, and accommodate yourself to the enemy until you can fight a decisive battle." #68: "At first, then, exhibit the coyness of a maiden, until the enemy gives you an opening; afterwards emulate the rapidity of a running hare, and it will be too late for the enemy to oppose you." Sometimes being over-prepared by over-analyzing, writing lists, reading self-help books and exhausted plausible methodology can ultimately paralyze you. As previously mentioned, by "over-preparing" in this way, sometimes your ego fills your mind with facts and figures to pull your focus away from action and into over-thinking. Moving into action with the "rapidity of a running hare" can effectively shake the ego strategist off kilter. Have you ever followed an intuitive inkling without delay, and found yourself

XII.

The Attack By Fire

1. Sun Tzu said: There are five ways of attacking with fire. The first is to burn soldiers in their camp; the second is to burn stores; the third is to burn baggage trains; the fourth is to burn arsenals and magazines; the fifth is to hurl dropping fire amongst the enemy.

2. In order to carry out an attack, we must have means available. The material for raising fire should always be kept in readiness.

3. There is a proper season for making attacks with fire, and special days for starting a conflagration.

4. The proper season is when the weather is very dry; the special days are those when the moon is in the constellations of the Sieve, the Wall, the Wing or the Cross-bar; for these four are all days of rising wind.

5. In attacking with fire, one should be prepared to meet five possible developments:

6. (1) When fire breaks out inside to enemy's camp, respond at once with an attack from without.

7. (2) If there is an outbreak of fire, but the enemy's soldiers remain quiet, bide your time and do not attack.

8. (3) When the force of the flames has reached its height, follow it up with an attack, if that is practicable; if not, stay where you are.

9. (4) If it is possible to make an assault with fire from without, do not wait for it to break out within, but deliver your attack at a favorable moment.

10. (5) When you start a fire, be to windward of it. Do not attack from the leeward.

11. A wind that rises in the daytime lasts long, but a night breeze soon falls.

12. In every army, the five developments connected with fire must be known, the movements of the stars calculated, and a watch kept for the proper days.

13. Hence those who use fire as an aid to the attack show intelligence; those who use water as an aid to the attack gain an accession of strength.

14. By means of water, an enemy may be intercepted, but not robbed of all his belongings.

15. Unhappy is the fate of one who tries to win his battles and succeed in his attacks without cultivating the spirit of enterprise; for the result is waste of time and general stagnation.

16. Hence the saying: The enlightened ruler lays his plans well ahead; the good general cultivates his resources.

17. Move not unless you see an advantage; use not your troops unless there is something to be gained; fight not unless the position is critical.

18. No ruler should put troops into the field merely to gratify his own spleen; no general should fight a battle simply out of pique.

19. If it is to your advantage, make a forward move; if not, stay where you are.

20. Anger may in time change to gladness; vexation may be succeeded by content.

21. But a kingdom that has once been destroyed can never come again into being; nor can the dead ever be brought back to life.

22. Hence the enlightened ruler is heedful, and the good general full of caution. This is the way to keep a country at peace and an army intact.

XII. The Attack By Fire

In this chapter, Sun Tzu outlines the best practices when attacking by fire and water. In many ancient traditions, fire is seen as a transformer and purifier. Cleansing your thoughts and purifying your intentions will serve to better prepare you against the trickery and manipulation of your determined ego. Then maintaining fluidity in your approach and your responses to your ego's attacks will ensure that you are malleable, ready and able to handle whatever situation may come your way.

1. #1: *"Sun Tzu said: There are five ways of attacking with fire. The first is to burn soldiers in their camp; the second is to burn stores; the third is to burn baggage trains; the fourth is to burn arsenals and magazines; the fifth is to hurl dropping fire amongst the enemy."* In many traditions fire is a means of cleansing, purification and moving forward. This is one of the final stages listed among the strategies in *The Art of War*. Thus cleansing and purification can be seen as one of the final stages in the battle with the ego. Do you feel ready to cleanse and let go of old habits, feelings or situations that no longer support your improving emotional health? Why or why not?

2. #2: *"In order to carry out an attack, we must have means available. The material for raising fire should always be kept in readiness."* To prepare for your cleansing, write

a list of resentments, individuals, past situations, judgments or character traits that you are ready to let go of and put behind you.

3. *#3: "There is a proper season for making attacks with fire, and special days for starting a conflagration. #4: The proper season is when the weather is very dry; the special days are those when the moon is in the constellations of the Sieve, the Wall, the Wing or the Cross-bar; for these four are all days of rising wind."* The "season" or best time for preparing this document is when you are ready to be open and honest with yourself. If you are feeling at all defensive, your ego is ready for attack. This would not be the time to prepare your list. On a scale from one to ten (one being "not at all" and ten being "very much"), note how prepared you are to leave your anger, sense of victimhood, judgment and bitterness behind you.

1———2———3———4———5———6———7———8———9———10

4. *#5: "In attacking with fire, one should be prepared to meet five possible developments: (1) When fire breaks out inside to enemy's camp, respond at once with an attack from without. (2) If there is an outbreak of fire, but the enemy's soldiers remain quiet, bide your time and do not attack. (3) When the force of the flames has reached its height, follow it up with an attack, if that is practicable; if not, stay where you are. (4) If it is possible to make an assault with fire from without, do not wait for it to break out within, but deliver your attack at a favorable moment. (5) When you start a fire, be to windward of it. Do not attack from the leeward."* At this point in the process, we suggest that you figuratively burn your list. As creating an actual fire could be dangerous, you could do a number of symbolic gestures to burn your list of past practices and

grievances. You may want to go through each item on the list, contemplate them one by one, and then cross each out after you reflect on it, seeing it disappear.

5. *#11: "A wind that rises in the daytime lasts long, but a night breeze soon falls. #12: In every army, the five developments connected with fire must be known, the movements of the stars calculated, and a watch kept for the proper days."* To be successful in completing this exercise in letting go of past habits, grievances and behaviors, you need to stay on top of your game, noting your responses to similar situations should they arise again in your life. Write a list of signs that would indicate that you are potentially stepping into potential trigger situations again.

6. *#13: "Hence those who use fire as an aid to the attack show intelligence; those who use water as an aid to the attack gain an accession of strength. #14: By means of water, an enemy may be intercepted, but not robbed of all his belongings."* Attacking the enemy with the use of water is more fluid and not as invasive as fire. In what situations would you benefit to be more fluid in dealing with your ego's outbursts? What tactics might you use that are more fluid?

7. *#15: "Unhappy is the fate of one who tries to win his battles and succeed in his attacks without cultivating the spirit of enterprise; for the result is waste of time and general stagnation. #16: Hence the saying: The enlightened ruler lays his plans well ahead; the good general cultivates his resources."* Are you able to think big? How far are you willing to imagine your life without the restrictions of your ego getting in your way? Take five minutes and imagine manifesting your desires into your life in a bigger and better way. Write your revised desire list.

8. *#17: "Move not unless you see an advantage; use not your troops unless there is something to be gained; fight not unless the position is critical."* Your ego can draw you into moving in directions that do not support your deepest desires—time wasters. Make sure that you are spending your time doing things that will affect your life in a big way. What "to-do's" are you doing that waste time? List them and make an effort to no longer waste your time on them.

9. *#18: "No ruler should put troops into the field merely to gratify his own spleen; no general should fight a battle simply out of pique. #19: If it is to your advantage, make a forward move; if not, stay where you are."* Are there any individuals that you antagonize because you simply find them annoying? Do you create drama or tension with them? If so, how? What can you do to prevent picking a fight in the future?

10. *#20: "Anger may in time change to gladness; vexation may be succeeded by content. #21: But a kingdom that has once been destroyed can never come again into being; nor can the dead ever be brought back to life. #22. Hence the enlightened ruler is heedful, and the good general full of caution. This is the way to keep a country at peace and an army intact."* In relation to your ego, according to Sun Tzu's wisdom, the dead cannot be brought back. Thus once you have destroyed your ego, it cannot return. This is good news. Sometimes we fear that we can regress, but each new insight cannot be undone. Each new experience cannot be negated from your psyche. Do you have any fears around the effort you are making here being in vain? If so, write about them.

XIII.

The Use Of Spies

1. Sun Tzu said: Raising a host of a hundred thousand men and marching them great distances entails heavy loss on the people and a drain on the resources of the State. The daily expenditure will amount to a thousand ounces of silver. There will be commotion at home and abroad, and men will drop down exhausted on the highways. As many as seven hundred thousand families will be impeded in their labor.

2. Hostile armies may face each other for years, striving for the victory which is decided in a single day. This being so, to remain in ignorance of the enemy's condition simply because one grudges the outlay of a hundred ounces of silver in honors and emoluments, is the height of inhumanity.

3. One who acts thus is no leader of men, no present help to his sovereign, no master of victory.

4. Thus, what enables the wise sovereign and the good general to strike and conquer, and achieve things beyond the reach of ordinary men, is foreknowledge.

5. Now this foreknowledge cannot be elicited from spirits; it cannot be obtained inductively from experience, nor by any deductive calculation.

6. Knowledge of the enemy's dispositions can only be obtained from other men.

7. Hence the use of spies, of whom there are five classes:
   (1) Local spies;
   (2) inward spies;
   (3) converted spies;
   (4) doomed spies;
   (5) surviving spies.

8. When these five kinds of spy are all at work, none can discover the secret system. This is called "divine manipulation of the threads." It is the sovereign's most precious faculty.

9. Having local spies means employing the services of the inhabitants of a district.

10. Having inward spies, making use of officials of the enemy.

11. Having converted spies, getting hold of the enemy's spies and using them for our own purposes.

12. Having doomed spies, doing certain things openly for purposes of deception, and allowing our spies to know of them and report them to the enemy.

13. Surviving spies, finally, are those who bring back news from the enemy's camp.

14. Hence it is that which none in the whole army are more intimate relations to be maintained than with spies. None should be more liberally rewarded. In no other business should greater secrecy be preserved.

15. Spies cannot be usefully employed without a certain intuitive sagacity.

16. They cannot be properly managed without benevolence and straightforwardness.

17. Without subtle ingenuity of mind, one cannot make certain of the truth of their reports.

18. Be subtle! be subtle! and use your spies for every kind of business.

19. If a secret piece of news is divulged by a spy before the time is ripe, he must be put to death together with the man to whom the secret was told.

20. Whether the object be to crush an army, to storm a city, or to assassinate an individual, it is always necessary to begin by finding out the names of the attendants, the aides-de-camp, and door- keepers and sentries of the general in command. Our spies must be commissioned to ascertain these.

21. The enemy's spies who have come to spy on us must be sought out, tempted with bribes, led away and comfortably housed. Thus they will become converted spies and available for our service.

22. It is through the information brought by the converted spy that we are able to acquire and employ local and inward spies.

23. It is owing to his information, again, that we can cause the doomed spy to carry false tidings to the enemy.

24. Lastly, it is by his information that the surviving spy can be used on appointed occasions.

25. The end and aim of spying in all its five varieties is knowledge of the enemy; and this knowledge can only be derived, in the first instance, from the converted spy. Hence it is essential that the converted spy be treated with the utmost liberality.

26. Of old, the rise of the Yin dynasty was due to I Chih who had served under the Hsia. Likewise, the rise of the Chou dynasty was due to Lu Ya who had served under the Yin.

27. Hence it is only the enlightened ruler and the wise general who will use the highest intelligence of the army for purposes of spying and thereby they achieve great results. Spies are a most important element in water, because on them depends an army's ability to move.

STUDY GUIDE

XIII. The Use of Spies

In this final chapter of his treatise, Sun Tzu shares insights on one of the greatest intricacies of warfare—dealing with spies. This is one of the most dangerous yet powerful strategic areas of battle. Being able to work with cunning and informed spies can be the strategy that can have the most profound effect on your army. How does the use of spies transfer to battling with your ego? Take care and use these players wisely as you embark on raising your army against your ego self.

1. #1: *"Sun Tzu said: Raising a host of a hundred thousand men and marching them great distances entails heavy loss on the people and a drain on the resources of the State. The daily expenditure will amount to a thousand ounces of silver. There will be commotion at home and abroad, and men will drop down exhausted on the highways. As many as seven hundred thousand families will be impeded in their labor."* Putting too much effort into your battle against your ego can exhaust you. Ideally, you need to take time off, when you do not focus on your emotional issues, but simply focus on whatever brings you joy. Write a list of things you really love to do. Then schedule at least one enjoyable event every week for the next two months. Then be sure to follow through on your scheduled "fun" time!

2. #2: *"Hostile armies may face each other for years, striving for the victory which is decided in a single day. This being so, to remain in ignorance of the enemy's condition simply because one grudges the outlay of a hundred ounces of silver in honors and emoluments, is the height of inhumanity. #3: One who acts thus is no leader of men, no present help to his sovereign, no master of victory."* Sun Tzu emphasizes being "humane" in your battle. Continuing to battle for years, exhausting your enemy is not humane. How have you been inhumane with yourself and others in your battle against your ego? Write a list, and then when you can, make amends for your actions or inactions. Be sure to do so with both yourself and others.

3. #4: *"Thus, what enables the wise sovereign and the good general to strike and conquer, and achieve things beyond the reach of ordinary men, is foreknowledge. #5: Now this foreknowledge cannot be elicited from spirits; it cannot be obtained inductively from experience, nor by any deductive calculation. #6: Knowledge of the enemy's dispositions can only be obtained from other men. #7: Hence the use of spies, of whom there are five classes: (1) Local spies; (2) inward spies; (3) converted spies; (4) doomed spies; (5) surviving spies."* Foreknowledge through the use of "other men" or spies is central to successful strategizing in this final chapter of Sun Tzu's treatise. While in the past we have spoken about having others in your life who support your personal growth initiative, it is not until you have reached the final stages of the battle with your ego, that you are likely ready to seek the assistance of spies. When you consider what spies are and how they are used, you can see them as an analogy in your personal journey towards greater peace. While Sun Tzu

lists a variety of spy types, they originated from within your camp, or within the enemy's camp and they all have knowledge that you need. Reflecting on your battle strategies thus far, are there any holes in it, or any areas of knowledge that you further require? If so, list them.

4. #8: *"When these five kinds of spy are all at work, none can discover the secret system. This is called 'divine manipulation of the threads.' It is the sovereign's most precious faculty."* What would you consider to be the "most precious faculty" in your pursuit of inner peace and self acceptance?

5. #9: *"Having local spies means employing the services of the inhabitants of a district. #10: "Having inward spies, making use of officials of the enemy. #11: "Having converted spies, getting hold of the enemy's spies and using them for our own purposes.#12: "Having doomed spies, doing certain things openly for purposes of deception, and allowing our spies to know of them and report them to the enemy. #13: "Surviving spies, finally, are those who bring back news from the enemy's camp."* Continuing with Sun Tzu's spy analogy, select individuals within your life that you could trust as your valued spies.

A local spy would be a friend or family member who is close to you and is "in the know" about the details of your ego challenges. You speak about your life's deeper issues, and he/she challenges you. He/she doesn't let you get away with ego-based trickery. He/she often offer you great wisdom and understanding that far exceeds that of others.

> Your local spy would be:
> Because

Your inward spy resides within you, however he/she is a member of the enemy camp. He/she has pre-disposal to the triggers, strategies and machinations of your ego leader. He/she is that part of you that is wise and immediately decides things and makes decisions without hesitation. Give this aspect of yourself a name and explain why you need him/her.

Your inward spy would be:

Because:

Your converted spy had originally sided with your ego, but has turned his/her back on the ego to support you. Is there a part of yourself that once was hostile, angry and critical that you recruited? If so, what is his/her name and why did he/she decide to follow your highest self? Similarly, is there an individual who you at one time considered your enemy that you were able to convert to becoming a trusted friend?

Your converted spy would be:

Because:

Your doomed spy does things openly for purposes of deception, and allows your spies to know of them and report them to the enemy. This is the part of you that is willing to accept responsibility and take the heat for your ego's misfires. He/she is willing to be completely exposed. Do you have a part of yourself that is transparent, or do you have a friend or family member who is brutally honest able their issues and yours?

Your doomed spy would be:

Because:

Your surviving spy brings back news from the enemy's camp. It is one of your soldiers who has been captured, and lives to tell of his/her experience. He/she has knowledge through experience. Is there a wise and experienced soul part of your-self that you can claim on your spy team?

> Your surviving spy would be:
> Because:

6. #14: *"Hence it is that which none in the whole army are more intimate relations to be maintained than with spies. None should be more liberally rewarded. In no other business should greater secrecy be preserved."* Whether individuals within your life, or within your psyche, these spies are of great value and need to be treated with the upmost respect and appreciation. They should be "liber-ally rewarded." How might you reward each? Be creative when you consider this question.

7. #15: *"Spies cannot be usefully employed without a cer-tain intuitive sagacity. #16: They cannot be properly managed without benevolence and straightforwardness. #17: "Without subtle ingenuity of mind, one cannot make certain of the truth of their reports. #18: "Be subtle! be subtle! and use your spies for every kind of business."* Sun Tzu suggested that you use "intuition, benevolences, straightforwardness, ingenuity and subtlety" when deal-ing with your spies. Have you cultivated each of these powerful traits within yourself? Which are you strongest at, and which need further cultivating? On a scale from one to ten (one being "needs a great deal of improve-ment" and ten being "very proficient"), rate your prowess in each area:

Intuition:

1——2——3——4——5——6——7——8——9——10

Benevolence:

1———2———3———4———5———6———7———8———9———10

Straightforwardness:

1———2———3———4———5———6———7———8———9———10

Ingenuity:

1———2———3———4———5———6———7———8———9———10

Subtlety:

1———2———3———4———5———6———7———8———9———10

8. Sun Tzu also claims that you can use your spy team for "every kind of business." Write a list of the ways in which you might use them beyond your battle with your ego.

9. #19: *"If a secret piece of news is divulged by a spy before the time is ripe, he must be put to death together with the man to whom the secret was told."* Being able to hold secrets and be trusted is a very important trait to master. Are you trustworthy with secrets? On a scale from one to ten (one being "not at all trustworthy" and ten being "completely trustworthy" rate how trustworthy you are in keeping secrets.

1———2———3———4———5———6———7———8———9———10

10. Have you ever broken someone's trust? How did you feel afterwards? Write about your experience and the lessons you learned.

11. *#20: "Whether the object be to crush an army, to storm a city, or to assassinate an individual, it is always necessary to begin by finding out the names of the attendants, the aides-de-camp, and door-keepers and sentries of the general in command. Our spies must be commissioned to ascertain these. #21: "The enemy's spies who have come to spy on us must be sought out, tempted with bribes, led away and comfortably housed. Thus they will become converted spies and available for our service. #22: It is through the information brought by the converted spy that we are able to acquire and employ local and inward spies."* So in this case, we must be able to charm, bribe or use whatever necessary means to lead the spy to our side of the battle field. What could you offer the aspects of yourself that side with your ego more than your higher self? Do you believe there is anything further that you could offer that would draw them deeper into greater peace over chaos?

12. *#23: "It is owing to his information, again, that we can cause the doomed spy to carry false tidings to the enemy. #24: Lastly, it is by his information that the surviving spy can be used on appointed occasions. #25: The end and aim of spying in all its five varieties is knowledge of the enemy; and this knowledge can only be derived, in the first instance, from the converted spy. Hence it is essential that the converted spy be treated with the utmost liberality."* Thus winning the loyalty of the enemy's converted spy is key to your success. Very often the people that often at first glance push our buttons, upon deeper knowing and understanding of them, we grow to like them. They convert from enemy to friend. Such is the case often with partners and even within us. If you look at the traits you most admired in the beginning of

a relationship, very often later, you find that trait annoys you. The opposite can be true as well. For example, you may be first drawn to a partner's laissez-faire, easygoing attitude, however in later years, you are annoyed by that attitude and wish they were more ambitious. Similarly, at first glance, someone may annoy you because they are outspoken and forthright. As you get to know them, you begin to appreciate and respect their honesty and fearlessness as a trait you admire and would like to cultivate more within yourself. Write about two such situations (one in which a trait you admire becomes one that annoys you, and another in which a trait that you first find annoying, becomes one you learn to appreciate).

13. In the situations above, why did you think your perspective changed? How might this insight help you to learn more compassion towards yourself and others?

14. *#26: "Of old, the rise of the Yin dynasty was due to I Chih who had served under the Hsia. Likewise, the rise of the Chou dynasty was due to Lu Ya who had served under the Yin. #27: Hence it is only the enlightened ruler and the wise general who will use the highest intelligence of the army for purposes of spying and thereby they achieve great results. Spies are a most important element in water, because on them depends an army's ability to move."* Reflect on where you were emotionally when you started reading this book and following the directives of this study guide. Do you experience more "fluidity" in your life? Do you find yourself better able to move through your issues in an easier fashion? If so, what were the key reasons why you've been able to shift your experience. If not, what do you believe is still getting in your way?

15. Now that you have completed reading Sun Tzu's The Art of War, do a personal inventory about the teachings and how you have integrated them into your life. Start by making a list of the new insights you have experienced as you set onto the battlefield with your ego. Write a list of what has worked for you, and what has not.

16. What steps can you take each day to further encourage yourself and support your efforts?

17. Write a list of expressions of compassion and kindness that you can give yourself to further nurture your sense of wellbeing as you continue to experience both the disappointments and victories as you continue your crusade on the battlefield.

18. Take a moment to honor yourself for completing this book and committing to your journey to defeating your ego. Reflect on all of the goodness that you have within yourself. Focus on all of the magical moments that you have contributed to enrich your life and the lives of those you have touched. Write a letter of honor and gratitude to yourself, and then read it aloud.